MELODY COLLINS THOMASON

The Magic Within

MELODY COLLINS THOMASON

The Magic Within

Cover by
Marc Sorozan

First published in the U.K. as
Miss Quarterberry and the Juniper Tree

Scholastic Canada Ltd.

ACKNOWLEDGEMENTS

'The Woods No More' from Jay Macpherson's *Poems Twice Told*, copyright © Oxford University Press Canada 1981; reprinted by permission of the publisher.

Dylan Thomas: *A Child's Christmas in Wales*, copyright © 1954 by the Trustees for the Copyright of Dylan Thomas; published by J. M. Dent & Sons, Ltd.

Beatrix Potter: *The Tale of Peter Rabbit*, copyright © Frederick Warne & Co., 1902. Reproduced by permission of Frederick Warne & Co.

First published as *Miss Quarterberry and the Juniper Tree* in Great Britain in 1989 by Orchard Books, 96 Leonard Street, London EC2A 4RH, UK

Canadian Cataloguing in Publication Data

Thomason, Melody Collins
    The magic within

ISBN 0-590-74313-9

I. Title.

PS8589.H652M23 1992   jC813'.54   C92-094367-5
PZ7.T484Ma 1992

7 6 5 4 3 2 1   Printed in Canada   2 3 4 5 6 /9
            Manufactured by Webcom Ltd.

For Jeff

Contents

We'll wander to the woods no more,
Nor beat about the juniper tree.
My tears run down, my heart is sore,
And none shall make a game of me.

JAY MACPHERSON

1

The Library

"R. QUARTERBERRY" said the three-sided name sign which sat primly on the counter at the library. Junie looked at it, mouthing the syllables of the strange name, and then looked up at the person who stood directly behind the sign. It was a tall, thin, weedy sort of person, wearing wire-rimmed spectacles, hair pulled back into a bun, long fingers busily riffling through a box of file cards.

Junie looked at the name again, and put her finger up to touch the indented white letters, feeling them with her fingertips. She wondered what the "R" stood for, thinking it would make for an exceedingly long name sign if it were spelled out in full, no matter how short the name beginning with "R" might be. For even Quarterberry on its own seemed a very long name to her, complicated and angular.

When she looked up again the tall, thin person was staring directly at her. This presumably, was R. in the flesh, looking severely through her glasses at Junie.

"Yes, Quarterberry," she said, as if Junie had asked her a question. "What is your name, child?"

Junie felt suddenly nervous and confused under that intent gaze, and she faltered, "Junie."

"June E.," said Miss Quarterberry musingly, saying it as if it were two words.

"No, um, it's Junie — "

"Juniper Tree."

"I'm sorry?" said Junie.

"Yes, Juniper Tree. That will do. What do you say, child? Are you an evergreen, or do you die in the winter?"

"I like the winter," faltered Junie, very much at a loss.

"Just so. Juniper Tree it is, then. That will be all."

Junie knew when she was being dismissed, and she was turning away from the counter when she remembered the books she was holding in her hand. She hesitated about facing Miss Quarterberry again, yet she wanted to read these books. She went back up to the counter.

"Excuse me, Miss —" she said in a small voice.

Without looking up, Miss Quarterberry answered, "Yes, Quarterberry," exactly as she had done before.

"Miss Quarterberry," Junie said the name for the first time. "I'd like to sign out these books, please."

At this Miss Quarterberry looked up, at last, stalked over to the counter and seized the books from Junie's hand, saying, "High time, too. This is, after all, a library."

Pushing her glasses up high on her nose, she examined the books, ignoring the library card Junie held out politely for her to take.

"Hmph," she grunted. "A horticulturist, I see."

Junie was signing out two books about gardens and magic. She had read both of them before. But it was summer again now, and she wanted to participate in the particular quality that summer shares with no other season. So she was reading these books again for the summer feeling of them, for their growth and greenness and moist fragrance. Junie had a strong sense of season; she took each one very seriously in its turn.

When she said, "I like the winter," to Miss Quarterberry, she was stating a conclusion which she had arrived at after much careful consideration of such things as snow on pine branches, the lights of Christmas, and the particular acrid, mothball smell of her winter coat.

She sensed the tone of condescension in Miss Quarterberry's last remark, and resented it, but now said simply, "It's summer," in what she hoped was a dignified manner.

At this Miss Quarterberry looked at her, and her face softened in an unaccountable way. Her mouth took on the shadow of a smile, a smile not contemptuous but gentle, and even her wire glasses seemed to melt and droop on her nose, endearingly askew.

"The child has a sense of decorum," she said to the air above Junie's head. And then, to Junie herself, "Well chosen, Juniper Tree," and she signed out the books briskly without another word.

Junie trailed slowly away from the counter. Miss Quarterberry had already turned away from her, attending to other things. The library was largely empty today, and unusually silent. The regular librarian, Mr. George, was nowhere to be seen. Though Junie had wondered at this when she first came in, she soon remembered that he had told her a few weeks earlier that he was going away on vacation, but that somebody would be found to replace him for those few weeks. Miss Quarterberry must be that replacement.

Junie remembered being sorry that Mr. George was going away, but also relieved at the word "replacement," for that meant the library would stay open for the summer. Sometimes no one was available, and then the library would close for several long, blank weeks, and Junie always missed it terribly.

It was very quiet. Even the two small children sitting on the floor beside the shelves of picture books made only the tiniest of sounds. They sat solemnly looking at books, slowly turning pages, a look of sober, adult concentration on their faces. Junie knew libraries were supposed to be still, whispery places, but here, in her library, Mr. George spread giggles like jingling pennies, and never tried to suppress them once they were started. His desk and the counter where you signed out your books were always a cheerful jumble of brightly coloured books and magazines, which he hadn't yet got round to putting away.

Glancing back towards the check-out desk, Junie saw Miss Quarterberry sitting there primly, writing with a long pencil, and could almost see "Shhh, shhh," written across her forehead. She just knew Miss Quarterberry liked a quiet library.

Junie didn't want to leave yet, even though she had already signed out her books. She didn't want to leave the rich, bookish, papery smell of the place, its inviting aisles of books. So she moved away from the children's room with its bright posters on the walls which caught the light coming in through the big windows, and started off towards the dimmer part of the library, where the rows of books made mysterious tunnels, the windows were smaller, and high, and dust motes turned slowly in the infrequent shafts of sunlight.

The library was housed in an old building, part of the small university in the town where Junie lived. From the outside it looked eccentric and peculiar, built partly of brick, partly of grey stone, with ivy clinging to its walls and an odd turret springing up out of the ivy here and there. Junie had heard people call it an "eyesore" and a "monstrosity" but it was, to her mind, perfect. It looked to her like a fairy tale castle, or a witch's house, and she was endlessly fascinated by the way it appeared both large and small at once.

The big open space just inside the entrance made the library cheerful and welcoming, but as you left that space it became shadowy, at times a little frightening. It had a tiny spiral staircase leading to an upper level, a staircase which Junie loved. There were long corridors walled with books, branching out into small rooms in un-expected places.

Junie had explored it countless times and yet there always seemed to be more, a corridor she hadn't seen before, or a new picture, or a chair tucked into a corner waiting for her to sit in it. So today, in the odd hush and quiet, she began to wander the place again, half exploring, half simply walking up and down the aisles in an aimless, dreamy sort of way, holding her books in one hand and moving very quietly in her sneakers on the polished floors.

Up one aisle she went, and down the next. Up and down. Along a corridor which led off at the end of one aisle, and back up it again. Up and down. Junie hadn't been looking at the books so much as feeling their presence (for she had a notion that they were half alive, and breathed, and whispered quietly among themselves on the shelves).

All of a sudden Junie noticed an opening at the end of one of the aisles, an archway which looked as if it might be the beginning of another of the branching corridors, and she thought, "I haven't seen that one before," and decided to see where it led. It did prove to be a corridor, narrower even than most of the aisles and hallways, and very dark. For just after the opening where it began, it turned sharply right and seemed to go on a long way. "Why, it must run along behind this wall," said Junie in the quiet voice which she used to talk to herself when she was alone. A single small light bulb dangling from the ceiling just inside the opening lit the hallway, but there were no windows that Junie could see.

Junie peered along the length of it, and could just make out, far away, a closed door at the other end. She began to walk towards it. And as she went, she noticed for the first time that this corridor was not lined with books as all the others were, but had instead a great many pictures on its walls. It was difficult to see them properly in the poor light, but Junie stopped once or twice and looked at the more interesting ones. Most of them were strange, complicated drawings in black and white, the like of which Junie had never seen before.

But one or two were proper paintings, colourful and quite beautiful. One showed a large garden in summer, full of blossoming flowers and leafy trees and elaborate ornamental shrubberies, with birds in its sky and maybe even bees in its blossoms. And there was a large evergreen tree right in the middle of the picture, and two people standing by it, a man and a woman. It was too dark to see what their faces looked like, but it gave Junie a funny, fluttery feeling in the pit of her stomach, the way she always felt the first day of school, or waking up on the morning of her birthday. She didn't know why.

And farther along, another painting caught her attention, a large portrait of an old man. At least, he looked old at first, but as she looked more closely Junie saw it was only his eyes, really, that were old. His hair was brown, not grey, and he had a short curling beard like an old-fashioned young man in a fairy tale might have. But his eyes were sunk deep in their sockets and deeply lined all around, and worst of all, they seemed to be no colour at all.

These eyes stared out at Junie from the picture as if they were alive, and she began to feel frightened. She hurried past the painting, deciding just to get to the doorway, try the handle (she was certain it would be locked), and then go home again. She barely glanced at the other pictures as she passed them, and at last reached the door.

It was a tall, narrow wooden doorway, and now she saw that, unlike the other doors of the place, it had carvings all over it, of fruit and flowers and birds.

Junie reached out to the polished brass doorknob and was just about to turn it when it turned of its own accord in her hand, and the door began to open inwards. She pulled her hand away and leapt back in surprise, dropping her books on the floor with a clattering loud thud. And coming through the door, with a brisk step and a positively radiant smile on her face, was Miss Quarterberry.

She wasn't looking at Junie and in fact didn't even seem to see her at first, until Junie let out a little "Oh!" of astonishment. Then Miss Quarterberry stopped, looked Junie up and down with a similar expression of astonishment on her face, and said simply, "Why, not yet, Juniper Tree. It is not yet time."

And then she began to walk away from Junie down the corridor. As Junie looked after her in confusion, still standing where she was, Miss Quarterberry spoke again, without slowing her pace or even turning her head, and in a completely different sort of voice from the one she had used at first. Her librarian's voice, Junie thought later.

"And for mercy's sake pick up those books, child," is what she said. "Show a little respect."

2

The Green Boots

Junie asleep dreamed of a dark place, familiar and strange at once. It was wooded, leafy, the daylight greens and browns strangely pale and unearthly in the moonlight. And someone was there. There was a faint crackling of twigs breaking underfoot, and a rustling of branches being pushed aside, as the someone crept through the undergrowth. The feeling of stealth, of furtiveness, came over her strongly. It was not like fear, though it had the same racing-heart alertness as fear. She struggled silently in the dream to see who made the noises, and caught for a moment only a glimpse of a pair of green boots. They seemed to be made of something soft and pliant like suede, the colour of mosses in moist woods. Soft-soled, they reached up high on the calves of the person who wore them. She looked up, straining to see the face of the wearer, and saw only branches and a play of moon-shadows as the leaves shifted in a light breeze. When she looked down again the boots were gone.

Junie woke with a start, halfway between fear and delight, blinked at the sunlight streaming through her window, moaned, rolled over, and tried to get back inside the dream. All she remembered clearly was the pair of boots, and she found that if she lay very still with her eyes closed she could call them up again in her mind's eye, could see their soft folds rising, could recall their rich colour, could almost feel them on her own feet, fitting perfectly.

But after a while, though she could still see the boots in her imagination, Junie knew the otherworldly feeling of the dream was fading, and she was trying to place the boots in the ordinary daylight world. It didn't work; she couldn't picture herself riding her bicycle in those boots, or going to school in them. She sat up, and sneezed as the sun tickled her eyes and her nose. Her cat, Willikins, who had been sleeping at the bottom of the bed, stretched hugely and put his paw over his eyes.

"Lazybones," said Junie, as she got out of bed. Willikins immediately walked up to the warm spot Junie had just vacated, and curled up to sleep again.

Junie pulled on the same jeans and shirt she had been wearing the day before, and went downstairs, where her mother sat drawing at the kitchen table, drinking coffee and smoking at the same time.

"Hiya," said her mother. "Did you make your bed?"

"Can't," answered Junie, pouring herself some juice. "Willikins is sleeping on it."

"That cat," said Junie's mother, smiling, and then turned back to her sketchbook.

Junie's mother's name was Fiona, a name that sometimes seemed to Junie very ill-chosen, not right at all, and other times perfect for her mother, just, and almost lovely. Her father's name had been — still was — Bob. He didn't live with Junie and Fiona any more. He left them alone when Junie was a very little girl, and though she couldn't really remember what he looked like, still she often thought of him. She remembered black hair, whiskers, and the smell of pipe tobacco when she thought of the word "father." Fiona never mentioned him.

When Junie was much younger she had had a confused idea that her father left because her mother's name was Fiona, and his was Bob — never Robert — and Fiona and Bob just didn't go together. Now, although she knew this was silly, still she looked at her mother sometimes and wondered why on earth she had to be called Fiona.

Her own name, June Elizabeth Summers, was a hand-me-down from her father's mother, deceased. It was her father who began to call her Junie, and now everyone called her that. She didn't mind; she didn't think about her own name very much. The problem of "Fiona" always seemed more interesting, beating out plain "June" in syllables, in sounds, in associations, in everything.

Now, however, Junie had acquired a new name, it seemed, in Juniper Tree, which Miss Quarterberry had insisted on calling her at the library. Junie was puzzled by it, but she rather liked it, too, and had carried around the thought "Juniper Tree" inside her like a special secret ever since the day before.

Fiona was not a professional artist, though she drew almost every spare moment she got. She supported Junie and herself by gardening in the summer, working in a greenhouse in the winter. "Freelance Gardener" was what she called herself, and the advertisements she put in the paper, the leaflets she had printed and distributed herself, went like this:

FREELANCE GARDENER FOR HIRE

"Have Spade, Will Travel"
The lilies of the field may toil not,
But I Do
For a beautiful, blooming garden,
tended lovingly and carefully,
CALL ME.
Reasonable Rates
NO LILY TOO LOWLY

Fiona had worked very hard at this, and was proud of it, refusing even to change the wording when one or two of her first clients had objected to what they called "an irreverent use of Holy Scripture for monetary gain."

"Irreverent! " Fiona had exclaimed to Junie at the time. "What on earth is irreverent about taking care of growing things? And as for 'monetary gain,' a person has a right to make a living, hasn't she? Irreverent!" The flyers stayed the way they were, and Fiona found new clients, people who were a little less religious, perhaps, but who had "more interesting gardens anyway," as Fiona said.

"Want French toast?" said Fiona now, smiling up at Junie.

"Really?" said Junie, pleased and surprised, and Fiona took that for an answer and got up from the table and began to rummage in the fridge, hauling out eggs, bread, milk. Junie sat down at the table with her juice and turned on the radio. She began to leaf idly through her mother's sketchbook, humming.

There was this about Fiona's pictures: they were all of clothing. She only ever drew with pencils on paper, and she always drew clothing. Usually she copied, from catalogues and fashion magazines, from whatever photographs had clothes in them that interested her. Faces would be edged in carelessly or not at all; clearly she was not interested in the people inside the clothes. Her pictures had as a result a curiously haunted quality, as if a ghost were to invade an endlessly varied closet and dress its invisible limbs in cloth of the richest texture.

"Texture" was one of Fiona's catchwords. Junie had heard her explaining to friends that this was what she was trying to embody in her pictures, and she would repeat the word with a kind of reverence: "It's the texture, you see," she would say. "Shape, form, colour — none of them is interesting to me next to texture."

And she usually succeeded. People who saw her pictures for the first time always reached out a finger to touch them, half expecting perhaps to feel cloth rather than paper. Evening gowns rippled liquidly across Fiona's paper, their silk almost whispering. Gentlemanly sportscoats bristled with tweed and leather elbow patches. Corduroy jeans ridged diagonally across the page, fading comfortably at the knees. And one wool cloak, Junie's favourite, looked both light and heavy on the page, thick but not clumsy, its wide hood falling gently over a half-finished face.

Their house was littered with sketches, sketchbooks half-full, half-empty, and pencils of every shape and size. Various glossy photos from magazines and catalogues were tacked up on the walls. And although these photographs had been copied in Fiona's sketchbooks, or were being copied, or were about to be copied, still they had an incongruous air there, with their smiling faces and bright colours. They seemed garish next to Fiona's pictures, loud and graceless.

"I have to trim Mrs. Hedges' edges today," said Fiona as she stirred batter briskly beside the stove. This made Junie giggle, and she repeated quietly, "Mrs. Hedges' edges, the edges of Mrs. Hedges."

Her mother looked out of the kitchen window. "Goodness, look at those tiger lilies," she exclaimed. "They really do need cutting back. They're taking over. What are you doing today?"

"Dunno. Want me to cut back the tiger lilies?"

"I'm sure that wasn't top of your list," said her mother. "No, leave them for now. I'll get round to them eventually."

The kitchen began to smell very good as the French toast cooked. Junie poured glasses of milk for both of them and got out plates and syrup, and soon she and her mother were munching French toast together at the table. Junie spilled some syrup on a sketch of a shirt, and looked guiltily at her mother, but Fiona only laughed.

"Never mind," she said. "I didn't really like that shirt anyway." She picked up the sketch by a corner and looked at it. "Too stuffy. It was coming out polyester, despite all my efforts at brushed cotton. How long will Karen be away?"

"Six weeks," sighed Junie. Karen was her best friend, and had gone away to her cousin's for the whole summer, or close enough. Junie felt somewhat blank about this so far, and was just beginning to realize how dull and empty the long summer would be without her.

"How about the library?" said Fiona.

"Went yesterday, remember?" said Junie, always surprised at her mother's absent-mindedness. Then she remembered her strange encounter with Miss Quarterberry, and said, "What are juniper trees?"

Fiona, taken aback at the sudden change of topic, raised her eyebrows and said, "Evergreens. Shrubs, usually, in gardens. We dont have any, but they're pretty common. Why?"

"Just wondering," murmured Junie, suddenly shy and hesitant to talk about Miss Quarterberry and the library; it all seemed so dreamlike, as if it were something she had made up rather than something that really happened. How could she tell her mother she had been called "Juniper Tree"? It would sound ridiculous, just as the green boots had seemed ridiculous when she tried to take them out of the dream and into the waking world. All the same, she persisted, "Are they always shrubs? Not ever trees?"

"Oh, trees too," answered Fiona as she gathered up the breakfast things. "It's just that you usually see the shrub kind in people's gardens. Shrubs are easier to manage than big trees, I suppose."

"Manage?" said Junie.

"Yes, you know, like what I do," said Fiona, suddenly capering foolishly in front of Junie, waving a dishcloth as if to wake her up. "Pruning! Trimming! Cultivating!" And she pranced about the kitchen, snapping imaginary shears in her hands, until Junie was helpless with giggles.

After breakfast, Junie went back up to her room to see if Willikins was still asleep on her bed. The bed, rumpled and empty, had a smudge of cat hair on the sheets, which Junie brushed off before she pulled them up and tucked in the corners. Down on her hands and knees, looking for a stray running shoe under the bed, she found Willikins again, curled up around the shoe, fast asleep.

"Sorry, I have to take your teddy bear," she said as she pulled the shoe gently from between his paws, and he blinked at her disdainfully, as if to say, "Teddy bear, indeed!" and then yawned and closed his eyes again.

Looking up after tying one shoe's laces, still uncertain about what to do with the day that stretched all sunny and empty ahead of her, Junie noticed that the light had changed in her room. The sun no longer shone directly into the window as it had earlier in the morning, but had moved out beyond the window frame, now sending its long rays into the room at a different angle. Junie watched its long golden fingers for a moment, philosophically reflecting, as she saw the dust motes turning lazily in the gleam, that any day now her mother would be telling her to clean up her room. Then she followed with her eyes the airy pathway the sunbeam seemed to make, and noticed that it was pointing directly at her desk where it sat against the wall.

Or more specifically, it pointed at the topmost drawer of the desk, the one where Junie kept all her most important things. This made her remember something, and she got up and went over to her desk and opened the drawer. She got out a book which was lying there, found a pen, opened the book to a fresh blank page and wrote: *Mrs. Hedges' edges* and then, underneath this, *The edges of Mrs. Hedges*. She looked at this for a moment and smiled, then shut up the book again and put it away in the drawer.

Junie's book, a smallish, lined notebook with mottled, stiff cardboard covers, was not really a diary. She certainly didn't think of it as a diary, nor would she ever claim that "Mrs. Hedges' edges" was an event, something that she did or that happened to her, like having French toast for breakfast. In her mind, the book was just The Book, and it was more of a place to her than a record. Like a treasure box, it was a place she put things she wanted to keep. For Junie collected words and phrases the way some children collect dolls or toy soldiers or coloured pebbles. Often she copied lines from books she liked, things that seemed to her strange, or funny, or beautiful, or true. One page, for instance, looked like this:

None of our camels can fly

Sailed on a river of crystal light
Into a sea of dew.

And then, feeling rather sick, he went to look for some parsley.
(A continually baffling sentence to Junie, who had never
heard of parsley being good for sick people, or even sick
rabbits.)

> *Come away, oh human child,*
> *To the waters and the wild.*

Would you like anything to read?

Here also Junie put things people said, things she
overheard, and sometimes things she thought herself.
Everfriend could be found on one page, which was what
Karen had christened her on the afternoon they pricked
their fingers with needles and became blood sisters. *Mrs.
Hedges' edges* now joined the ranks of Junie's collection,
jostling up against all the other interesting phrases that
murmured together in the dark desk drawer.

As she was standing by the window, looking out at the
garden and wondering what to do next, she thought
again of Miss Quarterberry, and Juniper Tree, and the
strange long hallway full of pictures. The thought gave
her a queer tingly feeling up and down her spine. These
three things: the person, the name, and the place, all
seemed to Junie to go together, to be connected with one
another. And then, she reflected, since *I'm* Juniper Tree,
I must go in there somehow too. And she wondered yet
again why Miss Quarterberry should call her such a

funny name, and why she had been coming out of that strange door, so far away from the children's room of the library, and what on earth she meant when she said, what was it? No time, or, no — "Not yet time," that was it. Time for what?

"Juniper Tree, Juniper Tree," Junie whispered to the tiger lilies out in the garden beyond her window. And they, as if in answer, waved gaily in a puff of wind. She was getting to like the sound of it, no question. And she decided that whether it meant anything or not, it deserved a place in her book. Cheered by this thought, as if it were the answer to a question, Junie went quickly back to her desk and took out her book again. She leafed through it, looking for a fresh blank page, and noticed something odd which caught her eye. Turning pages back and forth hurriedly, Junie found what she was looking for, and stared, astonished. For there on the page in front of her, in a queer spidery handwriting nothing like her own, were already written the words:

Juniper Tree

3

Marcus

Junie came clattering down the steps, two at a time, and Fiona called out from the kitchen, "What's all the racket?" Rushing breathlessly into the kitchen, clutching her book in one hand and her shoe in the other, Junie said, "I have to go to the library after all, Mum. I forgot something yesterday."

This was not exactly a lie, Junie reasoned in her haste as she plonked down on the floor to put on her other shoe. I did forget something. I forgot to ask that Miss Quarterberry what on earth she means by "Juniper Tree." For Junie felt sure somehow that the handwriting in her book had to do with Miss Quarterberry, or at least that Miss Quarterberry was responsible for it in some unexplained way.

"Why, you look positively harassed, Junie," said Fiona, standing watching her. "Why the sudden rush?"

"I'm making the most of my time," blurted Junie as she raced for the door, book in hand. "See you later!"

"Take your key!" shouted Fiona after her. "I'll be gone when you get back." And Junie dashed back to the hall table, grabbed her key, and ran out of the door again.

By the time she reached the little park which lay on her way to the library, Junie was completely out of breath from running, and found she had to stop in spite of herself. She stood on a green lawn with the birds singing all around her, and panted heavily. She could see the turrets of the library poking up beyond the trees on the far side of the park, and now that it was in sight, she was suddenly hesitant.

For she had no clear idea of what she was going to do when she got there. In her first flush of excitement, back in the security of her own room, she had considered nothing but taking her book to Miss Quarterberry, sticking it under her nose, opened to the page in question, and demanding to know how the words got there. But now that she found herself out in the sunshine, all alone, she suddenly felt a little daunted by the prospect of approaching Miss Quarterberry in such a manner. And she sat down heavily where she was on the grass to think out an alternative plan of action.

Sitting there, pulling out blades of grass, a frown on her face, Junie was retreating further and further from her first bold scheme. The next thing she knew she was startled out of her reverie by a sound of barking close by, and in a moment she had been knocked backwards onto the grass, and found her face being exuberantly licked all over by a half-grown brown and white dog. "Hey!" she cried out in a muffled voice through a tangle of paws and floppy ears. "Hey," she said again as the pup licked her right eyebrow, and then she was laughing.

Running towards her across the park she saw a boy of about her age, waving his arms over his head and shouting. She saw a glint of sunlight reflected off his glasses, and a leash trailing from one hand before she was knocked over again by the energetic dog.

"Victoria!" he called out sternly, or as sternly as he could while panting and pushing his glasses up on his nose and trying to untangle the leash from around his leg where it had caught itself. "Victoria, stop!" he commanded, and Victoria stopped. She sat down still beside Junie on the grass and gazed up at the boy with a sheepish look on her face, her long ears drooping.

"Sorry," he muttered in Junie's direction as he fastened the leash to Victoria's collar. "She thinks she's a welcoming committee to the entire world!" he added in an exasperated tone as he threw himself down on the grass to catch his breath, keeping tight hold of Victoria's leash.

"Victoria?" said Junie as she looked at the dog, who returned her gaze, grinning now, tongue lolling pinkly out of her mouth. "That's her name?"

"Yes, why?" returned the boy.

"Oh, I don't know," answered Junie, beginning to laugh in spite of herself. "She just doesn't seem like a Victoria somehow."

"Well, she does to me," said the boy, and he got up to go. But Victoria wouldn't budge. She sat firm on the grass beside Junie and braced herself as the boy pulled on her leash. "Come on," he said. But she didn't.

"I think she wants to stay," said Junie, and seeing the boy's confusion and embarrassment, she got up to go herself. "Bye," she said to the boy, and set off towards the library.

"Wait," he called out from behind her. "You forgot your book!"

Junie wheeled around quickly just as Victoria jumped on her again. Her heart had thumped horribly when she realized she might have lost her book — or almost worse — this odd boy might have picked it up and read it. He was holding it out politely to her now with one hand, his other arm pulled out as Victoria leaped clumsily after a white butterfly.

"Oh, thank you," said Junie. "I don't know what I — that is, I need it. Thank you."

"My name is Marcus," said the boy abruptly. "Did you know that one dog year equals seven human years, so that in a couple of years Victoria will be fourteen and older than me even though now she's only eight months, in our years, that is, which makes her — um, well, I haven't figured it out yet but anyway it's younger than me. So dogs can start out younger than you and end up older than you, which is kind of weird, don't you think?"

"Yes," said Junie, and couldn't think of anything else to say. "Well, I have to go now, Marcus," she said finally. "It's nice to meet you. My name is Junie. But there's something I have to do." She was very urgent in her need to get to the library.

But Marcus and Victoria followed her all the way

there, Marcus talking and Victoria barking, until they all reached the big glass doors together and saw the sign saying "No Pets."

Marcus and Junie looked at one another and then at Victoria, who barked encouragingly, eager to go in and welcome the library, the people in the library, and every book in turn. But Marcus said, "Come on, Victoria," and began to lead her away from where Junie stood on the steps, suddenly a little sad to see them go.

"Bye," she called out, waving to them. "See you!"

And Marcus waved back for a moment until Victoria jerked away from him and galloped off, trailing her leash, to greet an unsuspecting squirrel by a tree.

Once she was on the other side of the big glass doors, Junie went straight to the children's section, but Miss Quarterberry was nowhere to be seen. Other people, however, were everywhere. The children's room was positively crowded today.

Why, it's like a party, thought Junie as she gazed around, and at that thought, she realized all the people there were grown-ups, every single one. And they were not simply standing around talking to each other in the polite way adults do, they were also reading the books, and showing pictures to one another, and browsing among the shelves. Junie stared.

In one corner, three middle-aged men wearing business suits were sitting on the floor (on the *floor*, thought Junie) turning over the pages of picture books, much like the quiet children she had seen there the day before. But these three were far from quiet. They were talking to each other rather loudly, in fact, and comparing books with great animation.

Junie shook her head and rapped it gently with the heel of her hand to clear it. She thought she might be dreaming. Then she turned her head and saw Miss Quarterberry striding purposefully across the gap between one clump of people and another. Without another thought, Junie dived for the gap, hoping to find Miss Quarterberry there on the other side. Instead, she nearly ran headlong into a pair of elderly ladies, one with pinkish hair and one with blue, who were giggling together like a pair of schoolgirls.

"Oh, Agnes, don't you just love it!" gasped out the blue-haired lady. "The bit where he rides his bicycle right out onto the playing field? And then the green-haired witch swoops down and catches the ball right smack in her hands just before it knocks out all his spokes?"

"Yes, yes!" said pink hair. "But the poor elephant! Caught out again!"

At this point, the two ladies noticed Junie, who was standing listening to their conversation. She was wondering about the book they were discussing, and was just about to ask them its title, when they fell silent, eyed her with suspicion, and of one accord turned and walked away arm in arm.

Feeling a little hurt at this, Junie made her way towards the check-out counter, trying to ignore all the snatches of lively conversation she heard along the way. And Miss Quarterberry was there all right; Junie caught a glimpse of her busily stamping due dates. But then her view was blocked and she was rudely jostled away by a group of people forming a line along the counter, books in hand, talking and waiting to sign out their books.

Junie stood on tiptoe and strained to see over shoulders and peer around heads, for of course all these people were taller than she. But more and more of them seemed to appear all the time, and Junie, being small and easily overlooked, was simply shoved farther and farther away from the counter.

Junie retreated. She didn't know how to get to Miss Quarterberry, or even what she would say to her if she could — she looked so very prim and tight-lipped today. And she felt frustrated and a little foolish, as if she didn't really belong here at all.

She wandered away from the crowd, looking for a quieter place. Away from the children's room the library was quiet and hushed and its usual self. Junie sat down in a chair in a corner and opened her own book to see if the spidery words were still there. They were, bold and clear and inscrutable. She leafed through a few of the other pages, re-reading the old familiar words.

It was like walking into my own book, really, walking into that crowd of people just now, she murmured to herself. That's probably just how it would be if all the things I've copied here were all spoken aloud at the same time. And she smiled at this thought, because it seemed to give the whole strange episode some sense, make it understandable and manageable.

"I'll just go and have another look at that hallway with the pictures," said Junie aloud to no one in particular, and she stood up with renewed determination. A head poked around a book stack and said, "Shhh!" and Junie said, "Sorry," but she was smiling. It was good to be in a quiet place again.

She set off to where she remembered the secret hallway began. She reached Adult Fiction, as she had before, but when she went down to the end of the aisles to search for the opening to the dim hallway, she could find it nowhere. Nothing even looked familiar.

Catching sight of a door nestled in between the bookshelves, she hurried towards it even though she was sure there was no door yesterday, only an opening, a hanging light bulb. By now she had wandered quite a way from where she remembered the secret corridor lay, and she wondered at this a bit, but when she reached the door she caught her breath.

The door was like the grandly carved one she had discovered at the end of the hallway before. But Junie was too impatient to stop and look closely at the carvings. She took hold of the brass doorknob, turned it, opened the door and stepped through. And found herself standing outside in the sunshine, under the trees at the side of the library.

She turned around in astonishment towards the doorway, but it was gone. She was gazing at the blank, impassive stone wall of the library. A tendril of ivy trailed along it here, and a spider made its meandering way over the cracks. The wall looked as if nothing had disturbed it for years and years.

Junie felt a little frightened, and gazed up at the windows high above the ground, which merely reflected sunlight back at her where she stood. They reminded her of the sun glinting off Marcus's glasses earlier in the morning.

Glasses, glasses. Miss Quarterberry wore glasses too, the wire kind, plain, severe. There was something — Junie clenched her fists and closed her eyes and thought hard for a few moments. Yes! All those people today, every single one of them was wearing glasses too! And not just glasses, but glasses exactly like Miss Quarterberry's! That was why it was so weird, on top of everything else. How could she not have noticed it before? All those grown-ups with round wire glasses, like a thousand brothers and sisters of Miss Quarterberry.

She laughed at the memory of them, and because something joyful was bubbling up from deep down inside her. She knew this; this was exactly the same feeling she got when she read her favourite books.

"This is Magic," and she was speaking aloud again. "This is Magic, sure as sure. And I'm in it!" And she did a somersault there and then on the lawn beside the library, picked up her book, now full of the evidence of magic, the beginnings of it, suddenly precious and beautiful, and began to carry it gently towards home.

4

Mrs. Hedges' Edges

When she got home Junie was surprised to see it was barely noon. So much had happened, Junie felt like a completely different person from the Junie who had sat here at this table eating French toast just a few hours earlier. Her mother had gone to Mrs. Hedges' house, but had left her a note on the fridge door, held there by a large magnet in the shape of a fried egg. *Home by five, dear*, it read. *Sandwiches and fruit in the fridge for lunch. Love.*

At this Junie felt hungry, and she opened the fridge to find her lunch. There were tuna sandwiches there and salami with mayonnaise. Junie chose salami, poured herself some milk, and sat down at the table to eat, and to think things through a bit. She was restless with excitement, and kept shifting and bouncing in her chair as she ate. The sandwich, made of thinly sliced salami with lettuce leaves and lots of mayonnaise, all held together between thick slices of fresh bread, tasted delicious.

"This is about the best sandwich I ever ate in my whole life," remarked Junie to Willikins where he was dozing on top of the fridge. He raised his head and sniffed the air briefly, catching a whiff of salami, but was not sufficiently interested to move from his perch, and merely yawned at Junie by way of an answer.

"I have got to think," continued Junie. "I have got to work things out." But everything was simply a happy jumble of possibilities to her, and she couldn't seem to put it all together in her mind.

The library. Miss Quarterberry. "She's the one, it's all got to do with her, I just know it," mumbled Junie around a mouthful. "And all those funny adults today, it's like they were there on purpose or something." She chewed thoughtfully for a time. "On purpose to keep me away from her," she went on presently, "like that door, that magic door. I wonder why?" But to this question she had no answer.

She wondered if Marcus and Victoria were "in it" too. But she didn't think so somehow. They seemed too ordinary, too disorganized and chaotic, to be a part of Miss Quarterberry's magic. Even the mass of bespectacled adults in the library, with their chat and their books, seemed orchestrated somehow, next to Marcus and Victoria. "Orchestrated," repeated Junie aloud, pleased at the word. "Absolutely orchestrated." She wondered if she would run into Marcus and Victoria again some time and found herself hoping she would.

"Oh, I wish Karen was here," said Junie as she paced around the kitchen. "She would love this, she would just love it. And I want to tell somebody, to talk to somebody. Willikins, it's so exciting," she went on, stopping by the fridge and talking up at him, "but I don't know what I should do next. What should I do?"

"Why don't you go read a book or something," answered Willikins. "Some of us are trying to sleep."

"Oh my, oh my," gasped Junie. "Willikins, are you in it too?"

"In what?" answered the cat, stretching luxuriously where he lay. "So far as I can see, I'm not in anything."

"Oh, the magic, the magic. I'm in it, you're in it, you know what I mean."

Willikins blinked at Junie. "How do you know you're in it?" he said at last. "Maybe it's in you. Now go away," he said rather rudely, and curled himself up again with his back to her.

"But you can talk!" exclaimed Junie.

"It serves no useful purpose that *I* can see," intoned the cat with a weighty feline authority, "to state the painfully obvious."

"But you couldn't talk before," persisted Junie, reaching up a hand to stroke him as she had done a thousand times before, but withdrawing it at the last moment. This new talking Willikins didn't seem strokable, somehow.

"Now that," replied the cat, still speaking to the wall, his back to Junie, "is neither obvious nor true. I have always been able to speak. You, on the other hand, have hitherto neither listened nor understood." And after this pronouncement, Willikins refused to say another word.

So Junie finally did as he suggested, and went into the living room with one of her library books. But she was unable to concentrate for long. She got up to open a window. A breath of the mild summer air gusted into the room, bringing a scent of grass and flowers and the twitter of bird song from outside. The breeze blew a little stronger, and soon it was lifting and ruffling some of Fiona's drawings where they lay on the table by the window.

Two or three loose sheets were lifted right up by the breeze, and floated gracefully across the room like some new kind of rectangular butterflies. Junie let them fly until they landed, then went to gather them up again. The half-finished shirt from the breakfast table had to be fished out from under the couch, a little dusty.

On one of the chairs lay a straw hat with daisies on it, unlike the stylish things Fiona usually drew. Its daisies were askew and undisciplined, sticking out at odd angles, all looking as if they were trying to escape from the hat. It reminded Junie vaguely of something. Mary Poppins's hat, that's what it looks like, she concluded. But it doesn't look right without Mary Poppins in it. Lost, or something. And she wondered if her mother would ever start to put people inside the clothes she drew.

"There was one more. Now where did it get to?" said Junie, turning around slowly. There it was, on top of the bookshelf. She had to move a chair over and pile a few cushions on it before she could reach the corner of white paper she saw jutting out from the top of a jumble of books on the topmost shelf. She stopped to look at the sketch there where she perched, lost her balance, and came tumbling down onto the floor amid a confusion of cushions. But still she held the sketch firmly in her hand, and continued to stare at it.

It was a drawing of a pair of boots. Suede boots, they seemed to be. Soft-soled, they were tall, and would reach up high on the calves of whoever might wear them. They were the usual browny-grey pencil colour of all Fiona's drawings, not green as they were in the dream, but up in a top corner of the page, in her mother's small, neat handwriting, were written the words "moss-coloured, dark green."

Junie stared at the picture, awash in the memory of her dream of the night before. She had all but forgotten it till she saw the picture. But they were the same boots, all right, exactly the same. And this certainty came to Junie not so much because of the picture itself, but because of the powerful feeling that rushed through her as she sat there on the floor on the pile of cushions. Her heart was racing, a sensation of expectant alertness making her eyes and ears nearly tremble with attention.

She almost expected the boots to take on life, to walk off the edge of the page into some other world beyond the limit of the white paper. She felt she must not take her eyes from them or they would disappear, as they had in her dream when she looked away for a moment. For she was bereft when she discovered them gone, and she now relived that intense disappointment, that keen sense of loss, strong as all such dream feelings are, painful as a heart breaking, deep as a bottomless well.

Junie sat, oblivious to the room around her, watching the boots with longing and distrust, keeping her eyes on them for any signs of movement, any suggestion of fading, or change in colour. But her legs began to tingle and cramp after a while, sitting with them folded under her as she was, and she got up painfully, at last, her concentration waning, and put the picture on the coffee table. It was just a picture again. She knew it wouldn't disappear on its own. And only now did it occur to her to wonder how her mother should come to draw the very same boots she had dreamed about the night before.

Her light, joyous sense of excitement was gone. Looking at the picture as it lay innocently on the table, Junie began to think that perhaps she was becoming involved in something very serious indeed. Her heart was beating at its normal rate again now, but she knew that what she was experiencing, as she sat there, was neither light-hearted nor funny, nor even pleasant. It was a dark, hungry feeling, with as much awe in it as wonder.

She picked up the picture and carried it into the kitchen, intending to ask Willikins, in her most mature and serious voice, if he knew anything about it. But the top of the fridge was empty now, and though she looked through the house for him, searching out all his favourite hiding places, she couldn't find him anywhere. "That cat," she muttered, in a voice very like her mother's.

"Well," she said to herself finally. "Mrs. Hedges' house is only a few streets away. I'll go and see Mum and ask her about it." And feeling very calm and competent she set off with the picture in her hand to find her mother.

Mrs. Hedges' house was a five-minute walk from Junie's, in a very different sort of neighbourhood. The houses here were small, and rarely expanded up into second and even third storeys, as the houses in Junie's neighbourhood did. Rather, these houses seemed to hug the ground, and grow out sideways, if they grew at all, like creeping ivy next to the rangy hollyhocks that were the houses of Junie's street.

But Mrs. Hedges' house was different. Junie always liked to visit here, never quite sure what would be going on. From the front, the Hedges' house looked the same as the rest of the houses on the street. It had a white picket fence, a neat lawn, a few discreet flowers around the steps leading to the door. Junie approached the front of the house now and waved at her mother, who was clipping one of the shrubs in the middle of the lawn.

Fiona waved and smiled back, surprised to see Junie, but just as Junie came up, Mrs. Hedges appeared through the front door.

"Who is she today?" Junie asked Fiona in an excited whisper.

"Fay," answered Fiona.

And Mrs. Hedges came teetering along the path in exceedingly high-heeled white shoes and a fluttery pink dress, waving a handkerchief vaguely in Junie's direction as if she were a crowd of people a hundred yards away from her.

"Why, June!" she called out in an affected high voice as she approached. She was having a little trouble with her shoes, and wavered now and then, occasionally taking a few awkward steps in another direction as she tipped, as if her shoes had a will of their own.

"What a pleasant surprise!" she burst out. She clapped her hands together in an exaggerated gesture as she spoke, as if someone had just given her an unexpected gift.

"Hello, Mrs. Hedges," said Junie.

"Fay, my little pumpkin, call me Fay," insisted Mrs. Hedges.

Mrs. Hedges' real name was Gertrude, but few people ever called her that, maybe because she hardly ever seemed to *be* Gertrude. She was Fay, or Alice, or Samantha, or Mary Elizabeth, or one of the other characters she liked to pretend to be. She played. Alice was an overalled plumber who carried hammers in her pockets and clomped around cheerfully in heavy boots. Samantha wore only black — black trousers and sweaters, dark glasses — and smoked a cigarette in a long black cigarette-holder, balancing it delicately against her teeth with one black-gloved hand. Mary Elizabeth was a sighing, plump middle-aged lady with pearls and pastel dresses, always carefully coiffed, and always obscurely ill.

None of these characters was Gertrude, and yet somehow all of them were. There was a Mr. Hedges too, who stayed Mr. Hedges all the time. Which is not to say that he didn't play as well, for he did, but his games were different. Both Mr. and Mrs. Hedges were retired, and together had decided to spend their retirement doing what pleased them. To Junie they seemed funny, interesting and a little peculiar, but in a good way. Never old. Never even particularly grown-up. They were like outsized, mildly wrinkled children.

Mrs. Hedges, or Fay, after her elaborate greeting, leaned down close to Junie's ear and said in Gertrude's voice, "Would you like to come into the Circus?"

"Oh, yes please," answered Junie immediately, and

she forgot for the moment about the picture in her hand, stuffing it absentmindedly into a pocket as she followed Mrs. Hedges over to the red wooden gate at the side of the house. Fay looked around carefully to be sure no one was about, and opened the gate. Junie followed her through silently.

"Fore!" came a voice as soon as they were inside the Circus, and Mr. Hedges emerged from behind the windmill of the miniature golf course with a club in his hand. This he waved, smiling, at Junie, and then he proceeded to hit the ball through the door of the windmill, which set its wheel going and started a music box inside playing "Let Me Call You Sweetheart." Mr. Hedges waltzed himself around to the music in celebration of his success, and then moved on to the next hole, an elaborate water slide with tiny pool traps and dead ends.

The swings beside the trampoline beckoned invitingly, and Junie made her way towards them, stopping at the fountain to dip her hand in the water, which splashed down from a spout in the horn of a prancing stone unicorn. Fay by this time was kicking the gumball machine angrily, and she cried out, "Harold! Harold, this wretched machine has stolen my penny yet again!"

But Mr. Hedges merely called out, "Better call Alice and get her over to fix it!" At this point, the gumball machine made a loud metallic clump deep inside its belly and spat out one, two, three, four, five gumballs, and Fay laughed and clapped her hands in delight.

Everywhere Junie looked there was colour and motion. In the small spaces left between the swings, the trampoline, the golf course, and so forth, there were flower beds awash with bright tossing flowers, or tiny plots of grass in geometric shapes. These were the edges that Fiona came to trim and keep tidy. She had already finished with them today and the Circus looked neat, in a crazy sort of way, and cheerfully garish, and shiny everywhere.

Fay was trying, without much success, to juggle the five gumballs that the machine had finally given over to her. They kept falling and rolling on the grass at her feet, and she darted after them awkwardly in her high heels, her voluminous pink dress impeding her as she bent to collect them and try again.

The gate opened again and Fiona came through it, shears in hand. Fiona was one of the few adults welcome in the Circus. Mr. and Mrs. Hedges had a horror of their immediate neighbours, never invited them into the Circus, and spoke of them with a mixture of fear and contempt.

Fiona arrived at the swings just as Mrs. Hedges gave up trying to juggle and came over to offer a gumball to Junie. Junie popped a red one into her mouth with satisfaction. Fay looked at the other four in her hand, now melting their bright colours onto her warm palm, and then picked them up one by one and put them all delicately into her mouth. Junie watched, fascinated, as Mrs. Hedges' cheeks bulged in her thin face.

"Mrs. Hedges is going to have some topiary," remarked Fiona to Junie.

"What's that?" said Junie.

"It's training and trimming hedges into the shapes of birds and animals. You'd like it," said Fiona, and she gestured around at the tall hedges, as yet untrimmed, that screened the Circus on all sides from prying eyes and made it a cosy, secret place.

"Dall fullem," said Mrs. Hedges around a mouthful of gum. And then, seeing the blank faces that met hers, she held up one hand. After blowing a huge pink bubble that threatened to engulf her face, she pushed all the gum over into one cheek and spoke again, more clearly this time.

"Sorry," she giggled in Fay's high, girlish voice, somewhat at odds with her bulging cheek. "I said, that'll fool them! Imagine, green roosters and squirrels and robins, cones and balls and bushy bears. Why, Mrs. Battle will be nonplussed!"

Junie looked inquiringly up at Fiona.

"Confused," said Fiona, explaining. "Bewildered."

"Bewitched, bothered, and bewildered," sang Mr. Hedges' voice from somewhere unseen.

Mrs. Battle was the woman who lived across the street from the Hedges, and she took a strong interest in the Circus. She had never seen it inside, but its red gate and tall hedges roused a keen suburban curiosity in her bosom. She refused to participate in the lively characterizations of Mrs. Hedges' imagination, and called her "Gertie," which Mrs. Hedges could not abide.

"I'm finished for today," said Fiona to Junie. "Are you ready to go home?"

And Junie reluctantly left her swing and headed back towards the gate. Fay floated ahead of them and opened the gate a crack to check that Mrs. Battle was nowhere nearby, then waved her hankie at them as they passed through. The last thing they heard as they walked down the front path was Mr. Hedges' voice faintly singing, "I'll be seeing you . . . "

5

An Invitation

The next morning Junie slept late, tired out from all the excitement of the day before. She swam slowly up into wakefulness, remembering none of her dreams, but aware of a sense of pleasure and anticipation which she could not at first place. Then she remembered, and her eyes flew open and she sat up abruptly in bed, and looked around.

Willikins sat on the window sill washing his face. "About time," he remarked as Junie sat up. "Only the early cat catches the bird."

"Why, is anything special going to happen today?" asked Junie happily, relieved to discover Willikins could still talk.

"Am I a prophet?" replied the cat, pausing in his bath to look her full in the face. "Do I consort with gypsy fortune-tellers? How should I know?"

"I just wondered," murmured Junie in a hurt tone, "because you said it was 'about time' I was up. I just thought you might know something I don't know."

"I do," said the cat shortly.

"Oh, you do?" said Junie, taking this for encouragement. "What?"

Willikins blinked at her coldly. "I know many thousands of things you don't know, but among those many thousands of things there is not the tiniest snippet of information about what might transpire during the course of your doubtless uninteresting little day."

"I liked you better when you couldn't talk," retorted Junie, angry now.

"*I* have always been able to speak," replied Willikins coolly. And here he stalked regally out of the room.

"Beast," hissed Junie at his tail disappearing down the corridor, and then she tossed back the covers and got out of bed.

"Junie?" came Fiona's voice, calling up the stairs from below. "Are you up? The mail's just arrived, and there's something here for you."

"Is it from Karen?" Junie yelled back, excited to receive a letter, a rare thing for her.

"No. Come and see for yourself," said her mother's voice, fading as she walked away from the bottom of the stairs.

Junie dressed hurriedly and ran down the stairs. "Where?" she asked her mother, who sat at the table in the kitchen amid the usual clutter of sketchbooks, pencils, papers, and coffee mugs.

"Here," said Fiona, reaching over and picking up an

envelope, already opened. "It was addressed to me, actually, but it concerns you. Listen, I'll read it to you." Junie ached to snatch the letter and read it herself, but her mother had already begun.

"*Dear Mrs. Summers,*" Fiona was reading. "*It has become my habit, over the past few years, to make the acquaintance of the children who frequent the libraries where I act as summer librarian, in the relative leisure and unharried atmosphere that summer affords.*" Fiona raised her eyebrows in amusement, as Junie watched her, wide-eyed.

"Yes?" urged Junie. "What else?"

"Dreadful prose style," remarked Willikins, strolling into the kitchen. "Opaque, convoluted, tortuous."

Junie looked sharply at Fiona, but Fiona appeared not to have heard, and went on reading.

"*Accordingly,*" continued Fiona, "*having spoken to your daughter, June, on more than one occasion at the library, it would give me no little pleasure —*"

"No little pleasure," sneered Willikins. "The woman must be a Victorian."

"*— no little pleasure to receive her at my home for tea on Wednesday next, at four o'clock in the afternoon. I trust this invitation will meet with your approval, Mrs. Summers, and look forward to meeting June once again, on a ground less formal, perhaps, than that of the Circulation Department of the Public Library.* Phew!" said Fiona, taking a deep breath as she finished. "She likes long sentences, doesn't she?"

"Likes?" said Willikins. "Adores, more like, thrives on, lives and breathes, probably reads nineteenth-century sermons for breakfast!"

"Who?" said Junie to Fiona, trying to ignore Willikins.

She knew who had sent the invitation, she was sure, but still she waited, holding her breath, for the little space of uncertainty to be wiped out by her mother's voice.

"*Rosamund Quarterberry*," said Fiona, reading from the letter. "Or, sorry, '*Yours very truly, Rosamund Quarterberry, M.L.S.*' no less!"

"What's M.L.S.?" asked Junie.

"Many Lengthy Sentences," remarked Willikins. "Obviously."

"Master of Library Science, I believe," said Fiona.

"Can I look?" asked Junie.

"Sure," said Fiona, and handed the letter to her.

"Why bother?" said Willikins, lying at full length on the kitchen floor, and stretching his back paws lazily. "I'm sure it doesn't improve on re-reading." And then he put his head down and closed his eyes.

Junie stuck her tongue out at him and sat down to look at the invitation.

"Why are you sticking your tongue out at Willikins?" asked Fiona, who saw the rude face.

Junie reddened and muttered, "Oh, I don't know," and bent her head over the piece of paper.

"Poor old puss," said Fiona, bending to stroke Willikins behind the ears. "Has she been teasing you?"

"Intelligent woman," said Willikins as he inclined his head to show her where to scratch, but Fiona heard only his throaty purr.

The invitation was typed on plain white stationery. Miss Quarterberry's typewriter was evidently an old one, for the words were uneven in colour and every "r" jumped slightly above the other letters on the line, giving the whole page a strangely nervous look. "Rosamund Quarterberry" said the last line, and above it was a handwritten signature.

"Well? What do you say? Do you want to go?" said Fiona.

Junie looked up at her blankly for a moment, the spidery handwriting still dancing before her eyes. "Yes," she said at last. "Yes. Can I?"

"I don't see why not," replied her mother. "Has she been nice to you at the library?"

"Nice?" said Junie. The word didn't seem to apply to Miss Quarterberry.

"Yes," said Fiona. "Do you like her?"

This too required some thought. But Junie smiled, finally, and said truthfully, "Yes, yes I do." She hadn't realized it till this moment.

"Well, Wednesday next," quoted Fiona with the same amused expression on her face. "That's a week today. I imagine your social calendar can be stretched to fit in a tea party with Rosamund Quarterberry. What's she like, anyway? I'm curious about a person who still issues formal invitations to afternoon tea, in this day and age."

"What does she mean by tea?" asked Junie.

"Oh, ever so formal, my dear," said Fiona, affecting an accent. "Porcelain cups and saucers, small white triangular sandwiches, dabbing about the mouth," and she daintily touched a paper towel to the corners of her mouth to demonstrate.

But Junie was frowning. "I wish you wouldn't tease, Mum," she said. "She's not — well, she's just not like that."

And Fiona relented, seeing Junie's serious face. "Sorry Junie," she said. "Tell me, then, what is she like?"

Junie found this hard to explain. "Well, she's tall," she began, and then paused. "She wears glasses," she went on, and then didn't know what else to say. "She's — well, when she says something, you want to know what it is."

"OK, hon," said Fiona. "Maybe I'll get to meet her myself one day. She sounds interesting."

"Yes! Interesting!" exclaimed Junie, as if Fiona had stumbled on the right word for Miss Quarterberry at last. "Oh, I can't wait, Mum," she said fervently. "I just can't wait."

Back in her room again after breakfast, Junie took the carefully folded letter from her pocket and smoothed it out gently on her desk. Then she took her book from its drawer and opened it to the page with *Juniper Tree* written on it. She studied Miss Quarterberry's signature carefully, and then compared it to the writing in her book. "Hmmm," she said.

She rummaged in another drawer for a moment and soon brought out a large magnifying glass, one she used when she played Sherlock Holmes. From her wardrobe, after a bit of a scramble amid winter boots and shoes in the back corner, she retrieved the flap-eared deerstalker hat her mother had bought her at a rummage sale, and this she put on her head. It felt a little hot and scratchy, this warm summer morning, but she left it on all the same. She bent over the book, holding the magnifying glass up to one eye, then she bent over the letter, all the while crossing her other arm professionally behind her back.

"Hmmm," she said again, and she began to pace back and forth between her bed and her desk.

"No doubt about it, Watson," she said, waving the magnifying glass impressively. "These two . . . " and here she paused, casting about for the right word. "These two specimens," she burst out, "were written by the same person. The very same. The words may be different, Watson, but that particular way of forming the letters is unmistakable. Unmistakable," she repeated, and giggled.

She paced around her room a little longer, and then, warming to the game, paced along the hallway, down the stairs, and into the kitchen, where she examined Willikins' tail under the magnifying glass and tutted disapprovingly.

"It doesn't look good, Watson," she said. "Not good at all."

Willikins opened one eye. "Go away," he said. "Move to another planet. Inflict your childish games on someone more deserving." And he got up, stretched elaborately, and stalked away to the spot under the table where Junie couldn't reach him.

"OK, Sherlock, here's a mystery for you," said Fiona as she came into the kitchen carrying a large stack of papers and sketchbooks. "I've lost a picture, a new one. I only did it yesterday."

Junie gulped, and pulled off Sherlock's hat. "Hang on a sec, Mum," she said, and dashed back up the stairs to her room. She found the picture where she had left it, stuffed into the pocket of yesterday's jeans. It was sadly crumpled and smudged now, but even so, as she looked at it, smoothing it out as best she could, she felt an upsurge of the same strong feeling it had given her before. She shook her head quickly, as if to dispel the feeling, and hurried back downstairs with the picture.

"Is this the one?" she said in a small voice, holding the page out to Fiona.

Fiona took it, her surprise turning to displeasure as she saw the state the picture was in. "What on earth — " she began, anger rising in her voice.

"Mum, I'm sorry," burst out Junie, interrupting her, and she launched into an explanation to forestall Fiona's annoyance. She tried to explain about the dream, about dreaming the exact same boots, about rushing to Mrs. Hedges' house to ask her about the picture, about forgetting when she was invited into the Circus. None of it sounded very convincing, she realized as she was talking, and she trailed off lamely at the end, saying, "But I just forgot all about it . . . "

"Oh, Junie," said Fiona wearily, more hurt than angry now as she sat down, looking at her ruined picture. "You and your imagination. What am I going to do with you?"

"But it's true, Mum," protested Junie. "I did dream about them. I'm not making it up."

"I know. I believe you," said Fiona. "But it's just a coincidence, Junie. And that's not even the point. No matter how excited you get about something, you still don't have the right to destroy things that belong to other people. This picture was very important to me."

"I didn't mean to hurt it," said Junie, looking at the floor.

"No, you didn't, I'm sure. But you have to think, Junie.

You're old enough to know better. You have to be more responsible about the things you do." And Fiona left the room quickly, leaving Junie surprised and guilty. Never before had a picture seemed so important to her mother.

"But I just can't believe it was only a coincidence," Junie was saying to Marcus where he sat on a tree branch above hers in the park. They were well screened by the leafy branches from anyone who might pass by, and Junie felt pleasantly as if they were in a sort of green palace with living, moving walls. Victoria's leash was securely tied to a low branch of the tree, and she was dozing while Junie and Marcus talked quietly in the air above her.

Junie hadn't had the satisfaction of being punished for what she had done to her mother's picture. If she'd been denied TV, or made to clean out the garden shed, she would have accepted it, and felt she was making amends, somehow, to her mother. But the sight of Fiona's face was worse to Junie than any punishment, and made her feel small and mean inside.

She had wandered out to the park that afternoon, visiting the places where she and Karen most often played together. But the creek would not become a mighty river flowing into vast, unexplored lands for her, as it usually did. And the secret cave in the tree where she now sat had seemed at first merely uncomfortable and inconvenient.

She nearly passed it by altogether until she heard a voice calling her name from its shadowy depths, and discovered Marcus sitting high up inside eating an apple. Only now that she had climbed up to join him, and found herself telling him about the picture, only now did she discover to her relief that the tree was becoming a secret cave again, and that the land beyond the branches was once again an enchanted kingdom.

"Why not?" said Marcus.

"What?" said Junie, who had almost forgotten what she was talking about.

"Why don't you think it was a coincidence?" said Marcus.

"I don't know, really," said Junie. "It just felt like it all meant something, me dreaming about those boots and then Mum drawing them. It was sort of — creepy. I can't explain. It's just how I felt."

"A lot of fuss over footwear, if you ask me," said Marcus.

"But that's just it," said Junie. "They weren't like ordinary boots, like my winter boots or cowboy boots or the work boots my mum wears sometimes. They sort of gave you a feeling of, well, of magic," she finished awkwardly, afraid that Marcus would tease or sneer at the mention of magic.

"Oh, like seven-league boots!" said Marcus, interested again. "You know, in the fairy tale, the boots that can take you seven leagues in one step. Now those are magic boots."

"Oh, yes," answered Junie. "I've always wondered how far a league is." She was happy to hear that Marcus read fairy tales too.

"I'm not exactly sure," replied Marcus, frowning. "It's a long way, though. Longer than you can step, even if you're running. Like stepping over a whole town at once,

I think, or climbing a huge mountain in a minute. Like giant steps when a real giant takes them, only you don't have to be a giant to do it if you're wearing seven-league boots. That far."

"Yeah," said Junie slowly, thinking. "Yeah, I see. Tell you what," she burst out then suddenly. "Come over to my house and I'll show you the picture and you can see if these boots look like seven-league boots."

"OK," said Marcus, and he slid down easily from the tree branch where he was sitting. He woke Victoria as he landed on the grass beside her, and she jumped on him as if he'd been away for years.

Fiona was out when they reached Junie's house. *Mowing Mr. Simpson's lawn*, said the note under the fried egg magnet. *Won't be late. Love.*

"Sit down," said Junie. "I'll look for the picture. " And Marcus sat down on a chair with Victoria on the floor beside him. Junie went and rummaged in the living room until she came upon the picture of the boots. She felt a pang as she saw the sorry state it was in.

As she walked back into the kitchen, she was startled to see Willikins up on the counter by the sink, back arched, looking very angry indeed.

"Barbarian," he was spitting at Victoria. "Rude, ungainly, unkempt creature! Invader of civilized realms! Canine!" Victoria was trying to reach Willikins, wagging her tail but restrained by Marcus holding her leash.

"Willikins!" exclaimed Junie, stopping where she stood in the doorway.

Willikins ignored her, but Marcus said, "Willikins?

That's his name?" Victoria was now cowering behind Marcus's legs, and he reached down to pat her reassuringly.

"Yes," answered Junie, glaring at the cat.

"Hey, look," said Marcus, turning to Willikins and speaking almost as if he knew the cat could understand him, "she's only trying to be friendly."

"Friendly!" sputtered the cat. "One might just as well invite a blacksmith into a palace, a bull into a garden . . . "

"What a yowler," whistled Marcus in admiration as Willikins screeched at him.

"Let's go outside," said Junie hastily, and she herded Marcus and Victoria towards the back door.

"Wow," said Marcus, when they were safely outside in the garden. "A little touchy, isn't he?"

"You could say that," agreed Junie, embarrassed. Victoria had regained her composure when they came outside and was now licking Junie's hand fervently as if she had single-handedly rescued her from the dragon within. "His personality has kind of — changed — lately," Junie went on, feeling she ought to apologize for the cat. "I don't know why."

Marcus looked at her, his glasses sliding down his nose, then stretched out a hand and patted her arm.

"These things happen," he said gently, as if Willikins was an accident rather than a malicious monster, an eccentric aunt or mad uncle, an oversight, a mistake.

And then he changed the subject tactfully, saying, "Let's have a look at those seven-league boots."

6

Wednesday Next

The day of the tea finally arrived, after the week had passed more slowly than any Junie could recall. Fiona, making coffee in the kitchen that morning and humming to herself, looked up as Junie came into the room and burst out laughing.

"Is it a costume tea party?" she asked. For Junie was elaborately attired in her witch's costume from the Hallowe'en before. Her tall pointed hat, which she had made herself, sat darkly on her head, and crowned the black dress, magnificently ragged and dirty, the striped stockings, the old-fashioned black shoes, and various scarves and shawls which she had draped over herself to achieve a witchly swishiness.

Junie thought she was dressed appropriately for the occasion, which would undoubtedly be an unusual and magical one, and was taken aback by her mother's laughter.

"Junie, you'll frighten the poor woman to death," said Fiona, still laughing.

"Frighten her?" said Junie, who didn't think it would be possible to frighten Miss Quarterberry. In the end, though, at her mother's insistence, she went upstairs and changed into a skirt and blouse, neither of them black, both distressingly clean, and was obliged to content herself by practising fierce witch-like facial expressions in the mirror, and leering evilly at her mother.

"Don't you feel well?" said Flona, in response to one of Junie's contorted faces.

"No, I'm OK," said Junie, and found she couldn't hold the faces and talk at the same time.

The day crept by in inches. But finally, finally, Junie found herself walking slowly along the streets that led towards the address Miss Quarterberry had typed on the invitation: 13 Mulberry Street. Fiona had drawn Junie a map, since the street lay in a part of the town Junie didn't know well. Junie carried the map folded in the pocket of her skirt, but she had studied it so intently during the course of the day that she had no need to consult it.

As she walked, looking about her at the houses and gardens of the unfamiliar neighbourhood, Junie was imagining how convenient it would be to have seven-league boots like the ones Marcus had described. Then I could just step right out of my front door and be there, she mused, still unsure about exactly how far a league was, and wondering what you would do if you wanted to go only three leagues, or a league and a half.

"Wear only one boot, maybe?" she had suggested to

Marcus when they discussed the same problem the week before.

But Marcus shook his head. "Drive," he said. And then he'd changed the subject abruptly, Junie remembered, though she still didn't know why.

"Well?" she had said to him as they sat on the grass under a tree in Junie's backyard. "Do you think they could be seven-league boots?"

"Maybe," Marcus had answered, frowning at the picture he held in his hands. "Maybe not. Dunno. I don't like them, though."

"You don't?" said Junie, surprised. "Why ever not?" For she still thought them marvellous, despite the trouble they had caused between her and her mother, despite the small thrill of fear that crept up her spine as she looked at them even now. She gazed at them, fascinated, following their folds with her eyes, and said to Marcus, "I don't see how anyone could not like them. What's not to like?"

"They just — " Marcus said and then paused, holding the picture out at arm's length. "There's just something wrong. They give me a funny feeling, like when I know Victoria's tangled herself up in her leash when she's tied up outside, even when I can't see her. I know, and then I've got to go untangle her right away, in case she chokes herself or something."

"But I don't see what that's got to do — " began Junie, but Marcus interrupted her.

"Here," he said, giving the picture back to Junie. "Let's throw a ball to Victoria. I've got one here somewhere." And he rummaged in his pockets and found a small rubber ball, and began to toss it to a delighted

Victoria before Junie could say anything else about the boots.

"Rosamund Quarterberry," Junie was saying to herself as she walked. She was just discovering a way of rolling the unfamiliar name off her tongue in a convincing way, when she saw she had reached her destination.

Number 13 Mulberry Street was a spindly, ancient house, tall and narrow and mysterious. And it was so curlicued and ornamented, so turreted and twisted, so grey from its gables to its grey-curtained windows, that it had an oddly unsubstantial look, as if it was made entirely of gossamer. It reminded Junie of a flat line drawing in pen and ink, and as she walked up the path towards it, she felt like she was walking into a picture in a book.

But the brass door knocker gleaming in the middle of the door looked solid enough, and Junie lifted its heavy weight and knocked once, twice. Then she waited. Quietly she resumed saying "Rosamund" over to herself, and she started in surprise when she turned to find herself saying, "Rosamund" in a heartfelt tone to Miss Quarterberry herself. She stood in the doorway and looked at Junie with raised eyebrows.

"Correct, but impertinent," she said shortly. "Miss Quarterberry, if you please. Come in, Juniper Tree." She stepped through the open doorway and held it with an outstretched arm for Junie to enter.

"Good afternoon, Miss Quarterberry," said Junie and followed her inside meekly. Miss Quarterberry led her into the dark hallway.

"Have you been well, Juniper Tree?" asked Miss Quarterberry.

"Yes, thank you," answered Junie.

"If you will excuse me for a few moments, there are one or two small things I have to attend to. I will be with you again presently." And Miss Quarterberry's straight back disappeared down the hall.

Junie felt disappointment sinking and settling on her like a fog on a wet morning. Everything was so ordinary here, so colourless and flat. She looked around the hallway, noting with a heavy dissatisfaction the brown wallpaper, brown coat stand, and brown-curtained window by the door. Even Miss Quarterberry herself, wearing a plain blue dress and brown shoes and a gold chain around her neck, seemed no more interesting than anyone else, today. She seemed smaller, less sharply defined, smudged around the edges.

Junie sat down in a large brown leather chair which creaked loudly as she sank into it, and continued sighing for a long time as it swallowed her into its chocolate-coloured depths. Maybe there's nothing to it after all, she was thinking. Maybe Rosamund Quarterberry is just an ordinary, dull old librarian, who lives in an ordinary, dull old house.

She stood up again in a moment and went over to look out of the window. Impatiently she twitched aside the heavy curtain, but it was heavier than she expected, and slipped out of her fingers and fell silently back into its long concealing folds over the window. She lifted its edge again, and blinked painfully, for sunlight streamed into the hall through the window, shining directly into her eyes.

She blinked, and as her eyes grew accustomed to the light she found she was looking out onto a flower garden. She stood confused for a moment, staring out at the bright colours, the trees, hearing the bird song, and wondering when she had seen this place before, for she was sure she had. Then she heard a step behind her and turned quickly, dropping the edge of the curtain.

A small elderly woman stood before her, wearing a maid's black dress, white apron and white cap. "Miss Quarterberry says will you join her in the library," she said to Junie. And Junie, who saw that this was not a request at all but a command, followed the small woman as she led the way down the passage. This person, like the garden she had just seen through the window, looked strangely familiar to Junie.

The library must be a very long way away, Junie thought, for the maid led her silently along passages, up and down small flights of stairs, and around many corners. The house was much larger inside than it had looked from the outside. Imagine having your own private library in your own house, thought Junie with a small pang of envy. It made her think of a murder mystery game she played sometimes. Miss Quarterberry, in the library, with a revolver.

The maid stopped abruptly and Junie at that moment remembered where she had seen her before. She was one of the old ladies from that day at the library! The pink-haired one: Agnes, her friend had called her. Junie stared intently as the maid, with a cool politeness, opened a door for Junie to pass through. "This way, miss," she said to Junie, with none of her former liveliness. Junie caught a glimpse of pinkish hair curling out from beneath the maid's cap, and then the door was closed and she was alone.

Miss Quarterberry was nowhere in sight. The room was a large, well-lit place. The wall opposite the door had many tall windows, draped with blue curtains, all now drawn open and tied back to admit the light. And everywhere else she looked there were books. Books in glass-fronted bookcases lined every available bit of wall space, from floor to ceiling. A long table in the middle of the room was cluttered with books and papers. Books were piled on chairs and on the floor, in tall towers, tipping dangerously. There were paperbacks and hardbacks, books old and new, books in crumbling leather and books with bright pictures on their covers.

Junie wandered around the room in a happy daze, taking deep breaths of the library smell of the place. Too restless to pick up any single book, wanting to take them all into her arms at once, she began to caper around the room, half-skipping, half-dancing.

"Oh, Miss Quarterberry," she called out, lifting some of the papers on the table and peering under them. "Are you here?" she said to the air under the seat of one of the chairs, and, "Hey, Rosamund!" as she peeked behind one of the curtains. Suddenly she came to a standstill.

"Oh, dear," she said. For there in front of her was a narrow opening between the bookcases, an opening leading into a long corridor lit by a single naked light bulb dangling from the ceiling. "Oh, dear," said Junie again, and she stuck her head cautiously through the opening, glanced down the hallway, and pulled it out again. It couldn't be, but it was. The hall of pictures from the library, here in Miss Quarterberry's house.

"Now what do I do?" she said aloud to the bright, cheerful room in which she stood. But the bookcases merely gleamed silently at her, and the room seemed to hold its breath, waiting. Junie smoothed down her skirt and her hair, took a deep breath, and stepped into the corridor.

Everything was the same. Here were the pictures on the walls, the dim light, the closed door at the far end. Junie felt curiously calm and resigned now to whatever might happen, and she walked quietly towards the door. She stopped only once, to look at the painting she had looked at before, of the blooming garden. Just before she reached it she knew what she would see. She would see a painting of the garden she had just looked out upon from the window in the hall.

"Yep. There it is," she said as she gazed at it. "Well, she just had somebody paint a picture of her garden for her, that's all, or maybe even painted it herself. Nothing weird about that." But she was not convinced. The painting looked quite old, for one thing. And the tall evergreen tree in the middle of the picture had not been there in the living garden she had just seen. No tree, no people by the tree.

Junie shrugged, turned, and continued on her way. She didn't allow herself to look at the other painting as she passed by, the picture of the old young man, the man with the horrible eyes. She hurried past it, looking neither to right nor to left. When she reached the door at last, she knocked on it.

"Come in, Juniper Tree," said Miss Quarterberry's voice from the other side.

She stepped into a low, dark, dusty room. A fire was burning, making the place uncomfortably warm, but Junie barely noticed the heat. She did, however, notice the large black cauldron suspended over the fire, the blue and green coloured steam that rose from its murky depths and gave off a delightful smell, the broomstick leaning in a corner, but most of all, the witch who bent over a table by a small window, reading from a book and stirring something briskly in a bowl with an ordinary stainless steel egg whisk.

The witch straightened herself, her pointed hat brushing against a stuffed alligator that hung from the low ceiling, adjusted her round wire spectacles on her nose, and said to Junie, "Well, you've certainly taken your time about it, child! You were instructed to join me in the library, were you not?"

And when Junie said nothing in reply, but merely stood with knitted eyebrows, silently regarding the apparition before her, Miss Quarterberry spoke again.

"Why, what is the matter, child?" she said impatiently, even stamping one black-booted foot lightly on the stone floor. "Isn't this what you were expecting?"

7

Questions

"You have questions," said Miss Quarterberry, gazing at Junie from across the tea table. She was Miss Quarterberry again now, not the witch, but a cobweb still clung delicately to her hair, and a smear of dust smudged one cheek. She didn't appear to notice.

"I must apologize," she went on as she began to lay out the tea things on the table, "if I have frightened or confused you, Juniper Tree, for that was most certainly the least of my intentions. Or, at any rate, nearly the least." And here she set a pretty plate in front of Junie, a plate patterned with pink rosebuds and green leaves.

The tea table stood by the small window of the witch's lair Junie had entered. But the witch's lair, like the witch, was now transformed, and had become a comfortable small parlour. White lace curtains stirred in the breeze from the window, easy chairs sat by the table, and a kettle rather than a cauldron now simmered cheerfully over the fire. But the room was not altogether changed. The broomstick still leaned against the wall, the stuffed alligator still hung suspended from the ceiling, and the same books were piled on the mantelpiece, beside a large crystal ball on an ornate silver stand.

One of these books was the one Miss Quarterberry had picked up and leafed through hurriedly just after she saw Junie's face when she entered the room. "Oh, dear," she had said, much as Junie herself had done at the entrance to the corridor, and then she had read aloud from the book she held in her hand. Junie didn't understand the words she spoke, but she felt their power like something tangible in the room, spreading into every corner. The words seemed to hang and quiver in the air, to send their invisible vibrations into the very walls, into Junie herself.

And as the witch finished speaking and closed the book again, she did so with Miss Quarterberry's clean white hands, not the witch's clawed ones. And the hair those hands went up to pat into place was pulled back into a neat bun. And the person standing before Junie wore a plain blue dress, brown shoes, and a gold chain around her neck. But the eyes that looked at Junie were still the witch's eyes, the voice the witch's voice. These things, like the alligator and the broomstick, remained.

Junie sat in one of the easy chairs by the table and watched silently as Miss Quarterberry set out a tray of small white triangular sandwiches, a blue earthenware jug full of frothy milk, a platter of pink and green iced cakes, a large silver teapot, and a white bowl full of ripe strawberries. She placed a delicate cup and saucer beside

Junie's plate, and one beside her own. All her movements were swift and graceful and quiet. Junie's nose quivered as the warm red scent of the strawberries drifted over to her.

Finally, since it seemed to be expected of her, Junie spoke. "Are — are you really a witch?" she said in a small voice.

"Oh, yes indeed," replied Miss Quarterberry promptly, as she went over to the fire and lifted the lid of the tea kettle to frown into its depths. It didn't seem to burn her fingers, Junie noticed, interest rising in her again and beginning to displace her fear and confusion. "I should have thought you would have realized that by now, Juniper Tree," continued Miss Quarterberry as she strode back over to the table and sat down in the chair opposite Junie. "And I trust that you use the word in its widest and deepest possible sense, to imply a member of that noble company of makers of magic, rather than merely a bundle of clichés on a broomstick."

It took a few moments for Junie to digest this last statement, and when she had, she realized that she had indeed been thinking of broomsticks, black cats, and old crones with cackles. But she didn't know how to retrace her steps, so she said merely, "So — then you're not really a librarian after all?"

"On the contrary, I am a librarian as well," came the swift reply. "I make it a policy to pursue at least two careers in each lifetime."

Junie opened her mouth to speak again, but Miss Quarterberry wasn't finished. "The two professions are not so very far removed, one from the other." She spoke with her eyes half-closed, with the air of a professor imparting a valuable lesson. "Both are concerned with the care of books and their secrets," she nodded in Junie's direction, still with half-closed eyes. And then she gazed out of the window as if she had forgotten Junie was there.

Junie narrowed her eyes as Miss Quarterberry carried the kettle to the pot and poured boiling water into it. She was trying to see the witch again, to imagine Miss Quarterberry back into the black hat, the ragged dress which gleamed darkly with beetle wings, the high-buttoned black boots. This gave her an uncomfortable thought, remembering her own witch's costume, and she burst out, "Can you read minds?"

Miss Quarterberry looked at her for a long moment before answering. "No," she said firmly. "Do not fear that, Juniper Tree. I cannot read minds. Minds are not maps, to be held and read and comprehended so easily by another. I read books. I also read faces, which often give clues to a mind's secrets. And eyes, and smiles and frowns. A furrowed brow is as easy to read as tears rising," she said gently.

"I just thought," Junie went on uncertainly. "You said, I was expecting . . . "

"Weren't you?" demanded Miss Quarterberry.

"Yes, yes I guess I was," answered Junie. "But you just said you couldn't read minds. How did you know?"

"I can read faces, Juniper Tree. There is no magic in that. I can also see what books you choose when you come to the library. And I can see that when you turn your gaze upon something unexpected or unusual, you do not flinch or turn away, but look upon it with delight and curiosity. It was not so difficult to know what you might like to see, coming here today."

"Like?" said Junie.

"It was a — " Miss Quarterberry paused, and smiled ruefully. "It was a sort of jest, you see. I'm afraid I have a taste for theatrics that occasionally leads me to embellish to an unnecessary degree." And she sighed here in regret at her own lack of moderation.

Junie stared. A joke? It was a joke? She didn't know Miss Quarterberry *could* joke.

"So all this," said Junie, waving around at the room. "The cauldron, the spell, the hat — you were just — kidding?" In her surprise she was practically shouting now, angry all of a sudden, though whether at Miss Quarterberry or at herself, she hardly knew.

"Calm yourself, Juniper Tree," said Miss Quarterberry sternly. "It is not necessary to raise your voice.

"Everything you saw was real, and true," she went on presently. "The cauldron bubbles, the spell speaks and works its magic, and the hat — well, the hat is entertaining, but often rather awkward. Magic takes many forms." She lifted the teapot and filled Junie's cup. "In fact," she continued, "you might say magic is about taking many forms. Remember that, Juniper Tree; it is consummately important."

Junie eyed her teacup hesitantly; she didn't like the taste of tea. But she saw with surprise that it didn't hold tea at all, but hot chocolate. Its sweet, rich scent rose in a wisp of steam from the cup. She took a very small sip from the porcelain lip of the cup, gingerly. It tasted delicious.

"I anticipated that you might not be a devotee of tea," said Miss Quarterberry, observing the changes of expression on Junie's face. "It is, I grant you, an acquired taste. Once acquired, however, ever savoured." She now poured from the teapot into her own cup. Junie saw an amber-coloured stream of liquid flow from the spout.

"You will not object, I trust, if I indulge my acquired taste," remarked Miss Quarterberry as she added several teaspoonsful of sugar to her cup and stirred briskly.

"Can you have more than one thing at a time in a teapot?" asked Junie wonderingly.

"That depends entirely on what you put into it," answered Miss Quarterberry. But Junie didn't feel answered at all.

"Handsome, isn't it?" said Miss Quarterberry, waving one long white hand at the teapot. "Heirloom. Grandmother. Antique." She spoke in three short snaps like whips cracking, so that Junie thought for a moment the grandmother was the antique, not the teapot.

"Very pretty," she answered doubtfully, and looked down again at her cup as if unsure what she would find there.

Miss Quarterberry was holding out the tray of sandwiches towards Junie. "Cucumber and watercress," she said.

Junie took one and bit into it. It tasted cool and crisp and green, like biting into a spring morning. Miss Quarterberry refilled her cup. The breeze stirred the lace curtains at the window. Junie began to feel better and better. Questions were filling her mind, now, and she asked the one that seemed most pressing.

"Why do you call me Juniper Tree?"

"Ah, we come now to the heart and soul of the matter," said Miss Quarterberry, as if she had been waiting for Junie to ask just that question. She dabbed daintily at the corners of her mouth with a large linen napkin and helped herself to another sandwich and more tea from the multi-talented teapot.

"Juniper is strength, child," she began after settling herself once more. "It is steadfast, it is loyal, it is true and good. You are yourself, from tip to toe, from heart to skin. Juniper is strength," she repeated.

Junie looked confusedly at her hostess, who now munched energetically on a sandwich, eating with a gusto remarkable in one so ladylike. Then she looked at her own thin arms suspiciously, wondering what feats of lifting and carrying they might be capable of performing. Certainly they had never been particularly strong up till now. "But — " said Junie.

Miss Quarterberry held up one hand, still chewing.

"Do not suppose," she continued, after swallowing, "that I perceive before me, in you, an actual juniper tree, that I see you clothed in bark and green needles, planted in that chair as in a ten-inch plant pot."

Junie giggled and looked down at her own lap and at the chair she sat in, wondering how anyone could see her as a tree, of all things, even in fancy. But then, she reflected, never until today could I have imagined Miss Quarterberry all dressed up as a good, old-fashioned, warty, spell-making, broom-riding witch. And yet there she was.

"Do you know symbol, Juniper Tree?" said Miss Quarterberry.

This was so unexpected that Junie stopped smiling and looked up nervously. For a moment she thought of brass bands and loud marches, until she realized Miss Quarterberry had said "symbol," not "cymbal." "I think, um," she blurted out as if she was in school, "a symbol is something that stands for something. Like a flag stands for a country, or a wedding ring stands for being married."

"Precisely," said Miss Quarterberry, and Junie felt as pleased and proud as if she'd just written an examination perfectly.

"However," continued Miss Quarterberry, and Junie's face faltered again, "there is more. There is, with things as important as symbols, always more. For now, suffice it to say that Juniper Tree is a symbol for you. Its qualities — which is to say its essential and magical properties and attributes — are yours as well."

But Junie still didn't understand.

"In the days when magic was as common as marigolds," began Miss Quarterberry in a singsong voice as if she was telling a story, "in those days, juniper branches were burned when a child was born. The smell of the smoke, which is very strong and pure and sweet, prevented the fairies from coming and stealing away the child and leaving a sickly changeling in its place. Juniper kept fast the door, guarded the new-born babe, and with its own strength, ensured the strength of the child. Does your mother ever use such a thing as mothballs in a drawer?" she said in a very different tone.

"Yes, to keep the moths from eating the sweaters," answered Junie, startled into school again.

"Same principle," said Miss Quarterberry.

"You mean I'm like mothballs?" asked Junie, not at all pleased at this idea.

"No. You are like juniper. Is that not what I have been explaining?" said Miss Quarterberry, offering an iced cake to Junie. Junie took it gratefully, glad of an opportunity to look at something other than Miss Quarterberry's face for a moment. The sweetness of the small cake was comforting, and she ate it slowly, thinking.

"Juniper is an evergreen," said Miss Quarterberry after a pause. "It disdains the flighty deciduous habit of dropping leaves and dying off in autumn." She spoke as if all the trees that turned colour and lost their leaves were irresponsible, impulsive things, not to be trusted.

"And just as it retains its identity, its wholeness and integrity, throughout each season of the year, so do you," and here she pointed one long finger at Junie, "so do you remain yourself entire in every weather. In joy and in sorrow, with friends and with strangers, you retain a sure, strong core of yourself unchangeable within, like a light in darkness."

Junie was beginning, at last, to see what she meant. "So you don't mean," she said slowly, "you don't mean I'm sort of tall and green and stay in one place all the time. You mean I'm like a juniper tree in other ways, mostly in ways you can't see, but in ways that are important?"

Miss Quarterberry nodded, smiling. She held the platter of iced cakes out to Junie again. "Partake of another cake," she said encouragingly. "You are doing well, Juniper Tree. Symbol is deep and wide, child's play and metaphysics, the tool of both magician and poet. Juniper

Tree stands for you," she said once again, leaning forward over the table and looking deep into Junie's eyes. "And you, child, may also stand for the Juniper Tree."

She spoke so sadly that Junie felt awed and humbled, all at once, looking into those grey-green eyes, though she didn't really know what Miss Quarterberry meant.

And as Junie looked at her then, she thought she saw for a moment not the bespectacled, tight-lipped face she was beginning to know so well, but a beautiful face, a young face, shining with its own light, smiling warmly at her, arms outstretched in welcome and delight, looking at her as if she were the one person in all the world most loved, most wanted, most dear. Junie blinked and shook her head, and the vision was gone.

"It was a name of choosing, Juniper Tree," said the old familiar face. She brushed an infinitesimal crumb from the table, and spoke in an offhand way. "I chose it, in giving it to you. And you chose it, in accepting it. The magic binds very strongly, when two choose."

"Did I accept it?" asked Junie, who didn't see that she had either chosen or accepted the name in any way. She felt it had descended on her, like a sudden storm.

But Miss Quarterberry said, "Didn't you?" and regarded Junie steadily and intently once again.

And all at once Junie recalled the day she had stood by her bedroom window, looking out upon the garden, and whispering, "Juniper Tree, Juniper Tree," to the tiger lilies, to herself.

"Yes, I suppose I did accept it," she admitted at last. And then, looking up eagerly, she said in a theatrical whisper, "So it was you who wrote it in my book!"

"Yes," came the simple answer.

"How did you do it?"

"Magic."

"Wow," said Junie, much impressed.

"Your astonishment is gratifying, I'm sure, Juniper Tree," said Miss Quarterberry, "yet your own will effected the deed quite as much as did mine."

"My will?"

"Yes, indeed. You had to show willing. Had you not chosen to write the name in your own book freely, of your own accord, it would never have appeared to your eyes."

"Oh, sort of like invisible ink!" exclaimed Junie, thinking of the many secret messages she and Karen had exchanged, and then accidentally burned to ash over the flame that revealed the words.

"Something like that," agreed Miss Quarterberry, smiling slightly. "But your decision to accept the name was the fire that made the letters visible."

"So — instead of holding a page over heat, I just had to choose to write the name?" asked Junie, still unbelieving.

But Miss Quarterberry nodded. "The fire was in you."

In you. In you. Where had she heard that before?

In a moment she remembered, and forgetting for the moment about the mysterious appearance of the name in the rush of new questions that flooded over her, she said, "Willikins said that too. Did you tell him to?"

But Miss Quarterberry frowned, not understanding. "Who is it, may I ask, who has been encumbered with the unfortunate name of Willikins?" she said witheringly.

"He's my cat! Don't you know?" protested Junie, sure that Miss Quarterberry must be responsible for Willikins' new-found speech as much as for the handwriting in the book.

"I'm afraid I haven't had the pleasure," returned Miss Quarterberry, but she spoke as if making the acquaintance of Junie's cat would be entirely too much to ask of her, certainly more of a trial than a pleasure.

"But — he can talk, all of a sudden! He just started to talk, a few days ago. I thought for sure, you must be the one . . . "

"Who made him talk?" said Miss Quarterberry, finishing the question when Junie trailed off uncertainly.

Junie nodded. "He doesn't seem to like me very much," she added irrelevantly. "In fact, he doesn't seem to like anybody very much," she said after consideration. "But the thing is, when I was asking him, you know, if he was 'in it' — " and she said these last words in another of her confiding whispers — "he said, now what was it? — oh, yes, he said, 'maybe it's in you'!" she concluded triumphantly. "What do you think of that?"

"I think," said Miss Quarterberry, refusing to be cross-examined and speaking with infinite boredom, "I think he's very likely right. When did he begin to speak?"

"Why, it was," Junie paused, thinking back, "it was the same day I found the name in my book! Do you think it could have anything to do with that?"

"Do you?" said Miss Quarterberry.

Junie looked at her hostess for a few moments. "Do you mean to say," she said slowly, finally, "that I can hear Willikins because of the name, too?"

"I haven't said a word on the subject, that I can recall," said Miss Quarterberry, sounding very much like Willikins himself. But Junie knew she had stumbled on the answer, or been led there, unwittingly, by the apparently casual remarks of Miss Quarterberry.

"I feel," she said speaking more to herself than to Miss Quarterberry, "I feel as if I've been doing magic myself, making 'Juniper Tree' visible in my book, making it so I can hear Willikins talk — doing magic myself and not even knowing it!" She spoke with frustration, as if she had awakened to find she had slept through her own birthday party, or thrown away a magic carpet, thinking it only a rug. "It's as if I've missed it all," she concluded sadly.

"All? Scarcely," said Miss Quarterberry teasingly, and Junie looked up to find the angular face smiling at her once again.

She leaned towards Junie to explain. "You have acquired a new power of hearing, Juniper Tree. As to — Willikins — " (she pronounced the name as if it compromised her dignity even to utter it), "I would advise you to enjoy the pleasure of inter-species conversation, which will not be available to you for always."

"Enjoy?" said Junie. "But he — abuses me!"

Miss Quarterberry laughed. "Entirely churlish, is he? Well, then child, endure what you cannot enjoy. Among animals, as among people, there are always a few insufferable ones. The rest of us must simply manage them with kindness and forgiveness." She spoke with a complacent sense of her own charity that Junie could not let pass unchallenged.

"He says you have a dreadful prose style," she said, and waited.

Miss Quarterberry's eyes flew open wide. "He says what?" she asked in a frighteningly calm voice. Junie repeated what she had said. "Dreadful prose style?" began Miss Quarterberry, her voice rising angrily with every word. "What literature, I should like to inquire, what plays, poems, songs, sculpture — what art of any sort has the feline world ever produced? And this — this ill-begotten, bloodthirsty cat" — she spat this out as if it left a bad taste in her mouth — "presumes to aspire to be a critic of prose style?"

"Avoid him, Juniper Tree," she went on dramatically. "Scorn, ostracize, neglect, and banish the ill-mannered wretch! Put no stock in what he says . . . " She caught Junie's eye at this point, and checked herself abruptly.

"Ahem," she said, smoothing down her skirt and sitting down again slowly. "That is to say, Juniper Tree, I shouldn't concern myself about the beast too much, if I were you. Have a strawberry?" And she held the bowl out towards Junie with such a fierce smile that Junie snatched a strawberry as quick as she could, in case any stray claws should be exposed, and waiting to scratch.

Junie was trying to absorb everything Miss Quarterberry had been telling her. She glanced out of the window, saw with surprise the shadows lengthening, and got up suddenly, saying, "It must be late. I ought to go, I think."

Miss Quarterberry too, had been absorbed in her own private thoughts, and she seemed to look at Junie as if from a long distance away.

"Very well, Juniper Tree," she said, and she too rose from her chair.

"Thank you for the lovely tea," said Junie awkwardly, her hand on the doorknob. She felt, all at once, uncertain about the happenings of the afternoon, as if perhaps she had dreamed or imagined them. And for all the conversation she had had with Miss Quarterberry she felt no closer to knowing, really, who she was.

A kind of desperation took hold of her as she stood there by the door, a need to know that what had just passed was real. So she turned once again, and said, "May I ask one more question?"

"Proceed," said Miss Quarterberry in a tone not at all encouraging to Junie's mind.

"When I first came in here today," she ventured all the same, "what were you making?"

"Ah, of course," came the odd reply, and in the twinkling of an eye the parlour became the witch's lair once again, just as Junie had first seen it. The coloured steam was still rising from the cauldron, and Miss Quarterberry was bending over it, stirring it with a long-handled spoon. When she raised the spoon again something bright gleamed within it.

Miss Quarterberry gazed at it for a long moment, nodded her head in satisfaction, and carefully carried the spoon and its treasure over to where Junie still stood by the doorway.

"A gift," she said. "And a promise of a safe passage." Junie took the shining object from the bowl of the spoon. It was an oddly-shaped thing, like one half of a coin that had been broken in two. One of its edges was smooth and rounded, the other jagged and pointy like the teeth cut into a pumpkin lantern. But it shimmered blue and green like the inside of a seashell or the sky after a rain, and was perfectly smooth and unmarked on both sides. It was beautiful, and lay still warm and moist on Junie's palm like something newly-born.

"This too is a symbol, Juniper Tree," said Miss Quarterberry. "A symbol of a different sort. Keep it well. You may find it useful. God knows it no longer avails me," and a shadow of pain crossed her face as she spoke. The shadow passed, and she looked again at Junie, saying, "You will find your way home shorter than your way here. Come again tomorrow. Farewell." She opened the door for Junie to pass through into the hall of pictures. The tall witch's hat nodded encouragingly at her, and the last thing she saw before the door closed was the bowl of strawberries still sitting in the sunlight on the table like a huge red flower.

8

The Magic Garden

At the end of the hall of pictures Junie came out, not into Miss Quarterberry's library, but into the familiar aisles and polished floors of the public library. Junie wondered about that hallway as she walked home slowly through the park. Is it the hallway that moves around, or is it me? she wondered. Or both? But it flashed on her as she walked, the evening shadows dappling the grass and the wild flowers around her, that perhaps that hallway led into other places as well, other worlds maybe, if you had the right key.

All the evening, Junie was quiet and thoughtful, but every now and then, as she helped her mother with the dishes, or watched television, a large, bright, something wonderful would swell up inside her like a red balloon, and she would hug her knees happily, or smile a wide secret smile. As she was getting undressed for bed in her room that night she held the half-coin, the symbol, in her hand and wondered how best to keep it safe, as she had been charged to do.

For it seemed very precious and beautiful to her, and she felt she ought to guard it actively, not simply put it safely away in a drawer or lock it into her small metal money box. She touched its gleaming blue-green surface with a finger. It's like a piece of the sky or the sea, she thought. It really looks as if there is another half to it, as if there ought to be a bit that matches it and makes a whole circle. Like that part you cut off a boiled egg can be set back on to make a whole egg again. But never really whole, she thought then, frowning at the symbol. You can never truly mend a broken egg. Maybe this is like that too. The thought made her sad. In the end she laid it gently under her pillow and fell asleep at once.

But her dreams were troubled. She saw the green boots again, the boots standing in the dark, leafy place. This time their wearer began to run, and suddenly she was being chased by whoever wore the boots. The dream became a nightmare, a nightmare race in which she ran with sickeningly slow steps, legs heavy as lead, from this unseen pursuer. She could hear the steps behind her, the soft, heavy sound the boots made as they hit the ground in a relentless rhythm. They were getting closer. She couldn't get away from them, her legs wouldn't move. Just as she thought she would faint with terror, something in another part of her mind told her quite clearly, Change this, Juniper Tree. Wake yourself.

And her eyes were open on the familiar night shadows of her own room. She sat up in bed, still only half-awake, and looked around dazed as her racing heart began to slow down and beat normally again.

"Desk, chair, window," she said aloud to calm herself, naming the familiar things around her. "Curtains, clothes, bed." And then, as a pale unearthly light began to appear in the window, "moon," she breathed out, herself again. The half-full moon riding in the sky outside her window seemed a friendly, reassuring thing to her, a welcome face. She took the symbol from beneath her pillow and looked at it in the moonlight. It shimmered gently, its iridescent colours muted in the shadows.

"Look, moon," said Junie softly, holding the symbol out towards the window. "This one's only half-full too." She yawned, then, as the moonlight flowed silently into her room, and lay down again with the symbol against her cheek. And if she dreamed any more dreams that night, she could not recall them in the morning.

"I thought I would try to redraw them," Fiona said cheerfully, as Junie saw what she was drawing the next morning.

"Oh," said Junie, as she looked at the green boots taking form once again on a clean sheet of Fiona's sketchbook. She didn't know what else to say. The memory of her nightmare was still vivid in her mind, and made her regard the boots with a new sort of fear. But she was drawn to them still, fascinated. Almost in spite of herself her eyes kept drifting over to the picture as she ate her breakfast, watching intently as her mother shadowed in the folds of the boots.

"I have to go to the library," she said to her mother

when breakfast was over and the sketchbook closed up again.

"Again?" said Fiona. "You're spending an awful lot of time there these days."

"Yes, well, I guess I feel like reading a lot," said Junie, slightly defensive. She couldn't imagine her mother forbidding her to go to the library, of all places, but she wanted to be on the safe side.

But Fiona merely said, "Good for you," and Junie smiled. "I'll go with you today," she went on, and Junie's smile fell off her face like a cup from slippery fingers.

"With me?" she said, trying to sound casual.

"Yes. I need to get some books on topiary." And when Junie looked at her quizzically, she said, "For Mrs. Hedges? Remember?" Junie remembered.

There was nothing for it. She walked to the library with her mother beside her, fingering the symbol which she carried in her pocket and wondering how she could get to the secret hallway and the hidden room while her mother was with her. And what on earth would her mother think of Miss Quarterberry? "This is Miss Quarterberry," she imagined herself saying. "The librarian. Also the witch."

"You're quiet today," said Fiona inquiringly as they walked through the park together, and Junie smiled up at her and groaned inwardly.

As they passed through the doors of the library Junie hoped against hope that Miss Quarterberry would be nowhere in sight. But there she was, standing primly behind the counter and handing a book to a reader as if she disapproved of his choice of reading material, his style of dress, and his whole way of life generally.

"That's Miss Quarterberry," Junie murmured in an undertone to her mother.

And Fiona replied, "Is it now?" Junie saw the smile tugging at the edges of her mouth as her sharp eyes took in the tight bun, the plain, high-buttoned dress, and the pursed lips.

Miss Quarterberry glanced up as they reached the counter, so Junie was at least spared the task of attracting her attention.

"This is my mother." She spoke in a louder voice than she had intended, and all the people within earshot looked up from their books or their tables and took note that the pretty woman standing beside the little girl was her mother. Junie blushed furiously.

But Miss Quarterberry smiled a warm and friendly smile, and said, "Well, Mrs. Summers, what a pleasure!" and held out her hand to shake Fiona's. Junie saw her mother soften visibly, and stared in amazement as Miss Quarterberry proceeded to chat to her and charm her with dazzling smiles and friendliness.

"Thank you for being so kind to Junie," said Fiona in her best polite-to-strangers voice.

"Oh, not at all, not at all," protested Miss Quarterberry heartily. "We've enjoyed it, haven't we, Junie?" she said, saying Junie's real name for the first time and beaming down at her as at a long-lost daughter. Junie nodded dumbly.

In a moment Fiona had revealed her interest in topiary, and Miss Quarterberry had bustled off with her to help her find some books. "Ah, topiary," she was saying. "How absolutely marvellous! A dying art . . . so glad to hear someone . . . I know just the thing . . . " And they swept off together as if they'd been intimate friends for years, leaving Junie standing alone at the counter. She wondered what she ought to do next.

If I go to the secret hallway now, she reasoned, Miss Quarterberry won't be there anyway. At least, I don't think she can be in two places at once. It occurred to her that she wasn't sure. She had no idea of the extent of Miss Quarterberry's magical powers. But no, she decided, no, she couldn't be with my mother over there and with me in the secret room at the same time. But then she thought of the teapot which held both tea and hot chocolate at the same time, and became unsure again.

Her mother and Miss Quarterberry emerged from an aisle of books together and walked jauntily back over to the counter. Fiona saw Junie and beckoned her over.

"Rosamund has found me just what I need," she said to Junie. She was signing out several large illustrated books.

Oh, Rosamund, now, is it? thought Junie, and watched with resentment as Miss Quarterberry went so far as to chuckle, signing out Fiona's books.

"I've finished so quickly," Fiona went on. "Have you had a chance to find some new books yet?"

"Um, no," said Junie in confusion. She had forgotten that she usually came to the library for books.

"I have one or two special books that might interest Junie," gushed Miss Quarterberry, leaning her elbows on the counter.

"Well, good," said Fiona, smiling at her. "You don't mind if I dash home ahead of you?" she asked Junie then. "I'm dying to get right into these books with a cup of coffee."

"Um, no," repeated Junie. She felt things were going too fast for her. In a moment Fiona was heading for the door with her books, and she turned to wave at Junie and Miss Quarterberry. Miss Quarterberry waved back, and as Fiona disappeared, she turned to Junie and did the most astonishing thing Junie could imagine. She winked.

"Did you put a spell on my mother?" Junie asked indignantly when she and Miss Quarterberry were alone together in the small private library with the glass bookcases.

"Certainly not," replied Miss Quarterberry, all good posture and icy reserve once again.

"Well, you seemed to get rid of her in an awful hurry," muttered Junie.

Miss Quarterberry raised her eyebrows. They went higher up on her forehead than anybody's Junie had ever known. "I'll fetch the tea, shall I?" she said coolly, and she disappeared into the hall of pictures.

Junie wandered over to the window and gazed out upon the blooming garden, the one she had seen in the colourful painting in the hallway. It was only when she heard Miss Quarterberry's step behind her that she realized the garden shouldn't be there at all. She'd seen it from another window yesterday, the window in the dull brown hallway at the front of the house. "This garden," she said to Miss Quarterberry, gesturing towards the window.

"Garden?" said Miss Quarterberry eagerly, nearly dropping the tea tray. "You can see it?"

"Yes," said Junie, bewildered now by Miss Quarterberry's reaction as well. "But it keeps moving around."

"You can see it!" repeated Miss Quarterberry, the light she had bestowed so freely on Fiona returning to her eyes.

"Can't you?" asked Junie helplessly.

"No!" cried Miss Quarterberry, striding across the room and taking both of Junie's hands in her own. "Because it isn't actually there!" And this statement seemed to give her such pleasure that Junie was more confused than ever. She looked out of the window again at the bright flowers and the butterflies, and then turned back to see Miss Quarterberry floating several feet above the floor, doing a sort of crazy dance in mid-air. And as she descended to the floor again, stepping down as if she were walking down invisible stairs, she said, "It may just work after all!"

"Tell me, Juniper Tree," Miss Quarterberry said earnestly, "What do you see?" They were standing together by the blue-curtained window, gazing out at two entirely different views.

"But what do *you* see?" Junie persisted, still reluctant to believe Miss Quarterberry couldn't see the garden which lay so clearly before her own eyes.

Miss Quarterberry sighed. She didn't even reprove Junie for her impertinence. "I see," she began, "a plain empty lawn of grass (neatly trimmed and free of weeds, of course), but bare to me as an arctic waste, stretching away for a few yards until it is stopped by a row of tall, dull trees who stand there like so many soldiers, protecting me from the world." Her voice was low and solemn, and as she spoke, Junie thought the garden faded for a moment, melted away like snow in a warm rain, leaving only an empty lawn before her, an impassive row of trees.

Junie began to speak herself, trying to fill up the sad emptiness with her own voice. "But I see a beautiful garden, with lots and lots of flowers, all different colours. Oh, there's so much I hardly know what to tell you!" she said, turning for a moment to look at Miss Quarterberry's face, willing her to see what she saw. But Miss Quarterberry stood still as a rock, gazing in front of her with unseeing eyes. So Junie went on, trying to describe the garden as best she could.

"It's sunny," she said. "And there are butterflies, and bees at all the flowers. I don't know the names of all the flowers," she said uncertainly. "My mum would. But there are roses and petunias and snapdragons. There are paths going in and out, and big green shrubs all smooth like rocks with moss on them. And oh, I just noticed, way off far away, topiary! Like my mum's going to do for Mrs. Hedges," she explained and then realized that Miss Quarterberry knew that already. "I like that," she went on as she strained to see it in the distance. "Trees that look like animals, with leaves instead of fur. I wish I could see them up close," she said wistfully, and stopped talking.

She knew she couldn't describe the garden adequately. It seemed a charmed, delightful place to her, more lovely even than the loveliest garden she had ever seen. She longed to run out into it, to explore the paths and climb the trees, to see the topiary animals up close and touch their leafy fur.

"Well," she said finally, "it's just like the picture of it out in the hallway," and here Miss Quarterberry nodded, "except the big tall evergreen tree's not there in the front, and there are no people here. I wonder," she mused sadly. "I wonder that there's no one out there to enjoy it."

"But there is," said Miss Quarterberry.

"There is?" said Junie eagerly, looking out of the window again, half expecting to see children playing on the paths, perhaps, or someone pruning the roses. "Where?"

"He is hidden," said Miss Quarterberry.

"But if you can't see the garden," protested Junie, "and if you can't see anyone there, how do you know?" And immediately felt foolish for asking such a question. By now she ought to know that Miss Quarterberry had ways of knowing things without having to see them.

"Come and sit down, Juniper Tree," said Miss Quarterberry. And together they went and sat down opposite one another at the long, cluttered table. Miss Quarterberry cleared a space among the books and papers and set out teacups.

"When you say it isn't really there," said Junie confusedly, "what do you mean?"

"I mean precisely what I say," said Miss Quarterberry sharply. And then, more kindly, "It is not like other gardens, Juniper Tree. It is a magic garden."

"Yes, it looks like one," said Junie, looking out of the window.

"No, Juniper Tree," said Miss Quarterberry sternly. "Attend to me, please." Junie turned back to her with a start, feeling guilty. "I mean, Juniper Tree, that it has been made by magic. It is a concoction, woven with strong spells, to be sure, but nevertheless a bit of makebelieve, made of words and bottled powders. It is not there, because it has never been there. Not, at any rate, to the world at large. It was made," she said, almost painfully, "as a place apart, separate, private. It is like a secret room or a locked box, Juniper Tree. A place — a place where one or two might be alone, secure against intrusions. But as for being real, why, that picture in the hallway is more of a real garden than what you now perceive outside this window."

"But — but you know so much about it, Miss Quarterberry, and still can't see it?"

"I could see it once, Juniper Tree." She looked deep into Junie's eyes. "For I was one of those who made it. It was long ago, or if not so very long ago, say in another place and time. Do you understand what I am saying?"

"I think so," said Junie. "Like fairy tales?"

"Yes, like fairy tales," said Miss Quarterberry, smiling. "They never happened, and yet they are always happening." And somehow Junie felt she understood this too, for looking at that garden, she could easily believe in marvels all around her, and believed more certainly in Miss Quarterberry's magic now than she had when faced with the tall hat and the cauldron.

"Why," said Junie softly, aware that she was treading on dangerous ground, "why can't you see it now, Miss Quarterberry?" For it seemed all at once the saddest thing in the world to her that Miss Quarterberry should be deprived of this beautiful place she had made.

"Say, rather, child, why is it you can?" Miss Quarterberry got up and walked up and down the room, her fingertips pressed together in front of her lips, silent and absorbed. Junie glanced down at the smooth tabletop, and saw a pale reflection there of her own face. It looked very white and young and silly, and she turned her eyes away at once.

Miss Quarterberry turned at the window and walked back towards Junie. Junie saw, with only the merest start of surprise, that she held a framed picture in her long white hands. The picture from the hallway. And as Junie looked up expectantly to see the picture of the garden once again, she was startled by the haggard face of the man staring at her from inside the frame, for all the world as if he was alive.

Junie flinched, and gave a little cry at being taken so cruelly by surprise by the portrait. She looked up at Miss Quarterberry reproachfully, but Miss Quarterberry said, "Don't be frightened, Juniper Tree. This is the one who inhabits the magic garden."

The eyes gazed balefully at Junie from the picture, and she was seized with terror. She looked wildly from the horrible face to the beautiful garden, and cried, "Oh, no!" The room swam around her for a moment, and she felt as if she might faint, but she felt Miss Quarterberry's hands gentle on her shoulders, helping her up and leading her down the hall of pictures and into the small parlour. "Oh, dear," she heard Miss Quarterberry say, and then her legs turned to water beneath her and the light disappeared altogether.

When she opened her eyes Junie found herself lying on a small couch by the fireplace in the parlour. Miss Quarterberry was sitting in a chair near her, her pale face tight with concern as she leaned over Junie. Seeing that thin, plain face looking at her as if she were a sick kitten, Junie smiled in spite of herself. Miss Quarterberry smiled back at her, and in that moment they ceased to be small girl and grown woman, child and librarian, impertinent and reproving. They became friends, then, companionable and affectionate, and something of that warm, shared smile remained between them forever afterwards, even when Junie shrank back into a small girl once again, and Miss Quarterberry resumed the angular, unpredictable proportions that Junie found so curious and so exasperating.

"Has that man taken your garden from you, Miss Quarterberry?" asked Junie.

"In a way, Juniper Tree, in a way," answered Miss Quarterberry, standing up and beginning to pace slowly up and down the small room. "I must confess," she continued, "I had hoped you would eventually learn to see the garden, Juniper Tree. I did not know it would be in you to see it so soon, or so completely. For it is in you, you understand, child," she said, looking at Junie. "It is none of my doing."

"In me?" asked Junie. "Why can I see it? Can't anybody else?"

"Occasionally a person passing by will hear a trill of bird song, but see no bird, or smell spring blossoms in midsummer . . . the garden is so full of magic, it is like an ocean in a saucer. It can't help but leak, sometimes. It — just leaks, from abundance, as blossoms fall to the ground in the spring, under the weight of their own white petals."

Junie thought for a moment of herself, slopping milk, slopping juice from glasses at home. But if a magic garden could leak like that . . . why, you'd hope for constant clumsiness, for little drops of the magic to come falling out of the garden, always.

Miss Quarterberry spoke with a strange half-smile on her face. "Once a woman found the pavement littered with June rose petals, as she sped past the garden on a chill evening in November. She gathered them up into a handkerchief, and took them home, and put them into a drawer for the scent. Now," said Miss Quarterberry, her face pursed up so strangely that Junie did not at first realize she was suppressing laughter, "now the underwear in that drawer will last forever, and carry with it always the scent of new roses."

Now Junie too was trying not to laugh. "Does she know?" she asked.

"She thinks only," said Miss Quarterberry, laughing now in spite of herself, "that they made undergarments of a quality exceedingly fine when she was a girl, and laments the inferior workmanship of today."

They were laughing together now. Their laughter faded slowly, like the light from a summer evening, and when they were calm again Miss Quarterberry said, "But you are the first, child, the first in the many, many long years since the garden disappeared from me, the first to see it truly, to see it whole, from the outside."

And all at once, Junie felt a little lonely and daunted. She didn't want to be the only one who could see the garden. It made her feel responsible for it, somehow, and she shrank from such a responsibility, seeing and knowing about such a beautiful, powerful place.

"But how come it's me? I don't see — "

"But you do see," interrupted Miss Quarterberry. And then she went on in gentler tones. "I don't truly know, child, why you see it when I cannot, when it has been sealed off and shut away like a vision of paradise. But I do know that it is in you, a magic and a power of knowing that you carry within you. I saw it glowing in your eyes like embers when you first approached me in the library. Seeing it, knowing it for the power it was, I named it, and you. Since the naming it has, I think, begun to stir within you, to know itself, to give you a seeing vision which you did not know you had."

"Like hearing Willikins?" asked Junie. "Is it a new seeing like that new hearing?"

"Indeed, child. And perhaps, perhaps the naming of the magic within you brought it into life, wakened it, allowed your eyes to see the wonders that others cannot. But only you, Juniper Tree, only you can search your soul and say whether or not I speak truly. The magic lies in your heart. I named it, but you possess it."

Junie sat silent, looking down at her own hands in her lap, overwhelmed by the things Miss Quarterberry was telling her. She was half-thrilled, half-terrified at the thought of this magic she was supposed to possess, and she was beginning to realize that she was indeed alone, more alone than she had ever been before. She was beginning to feel a loneliness that has nothing to do with how many people there are in a room with you. It had to do with seeing the garden, the garden she felt she could gaze at forever in longing and delight, and yet knowing that Miss Quarterberry could not see it, could not share it. She almost felt that *she* was the one robbing Miss Quarterberry of her garden, simply by being the only one able to see it. But this thought upset her so much that she shook her head to dispel it.

Miss Quarterberry meanwhile had been busying herself in a corner of the room, and she came towards Junie now carrying a beautiful golden goblet, steaming blue and green like the cauldron had the day before.

"Drink this, Juniper Tree," she said, holding the goblet out towards Junie. "It will refresh you."

Junie took the goblet and peered into its depths rather nervously. "What — what is it?" she asked, not wanting to be rude, but hesitant all the same to taste this witchly brew which smelled like nothing else she had ever encountered.

"What?" snapped Miss Quarterberry. "You will refuse the first (and possibly last) magical potion ever offered you? You would prefer chicken soup, perhaps?" She clapped her hands sharply in Junie's direction, and all at once the steam from the goblet paled, and smelt most suddenly and unmistakably of chicken soup. Junie gazed at the goblet wonderingly.

"Cranberry juice?" clapped Miss Quarterberry, and the goblet went cold in Junie's hands, the steam disappeared abruptly, and a clear red liquid lapped gently at its edges.

"Coffee?" And the goblet smelled of Junie's kitchen at home in the morning.

"OK, OK," she protested. "I'm sorry. Please stop."

And the goblet once again held the magical potion. Junie looked at it ruefully, looked at Miss Quarterberry, who stood frowning at her, took a deep breath, and drank.

It tasted of cold, pure water at first, but as she swallowed, Junie discerned several other flavours in it as well, none of which she could name.

"Distilled sunlight," said Miss Quarterberry, as Junie drained the goblet. "Spring water, rose-hip nectar, rain caught in rose petals at evening, morning dew in new grass, a small amount of mead (so as not to intoxicate a minor), and one or two other essences for the refreshment of body and spirit."

Junie set the empty goblet carefully on the low table. She felt marvellous, as if she had just awakened after a long sleep full of sweet dreams, swum in a clear pool, and eaten a wonderful dinner with her mother, all at once. She was curious about the "one or two other essences" which she felt sure were the heart and soul of the potion she had just drunk, but Miss Quarterberry had snapped out the list of ingredients in such a sharp, offended manner that she felt she dare not ask about them.

"Thank you, Miss Quarterberry," she said instead, sweetly. "It was delicious."

"Juniper Tree," said Miss Quarterberry, her volatile mood settling into calm seriousness once again. "I have a very great thing to ask of you." Junie looked up nervously, her own mood shifting as suddenly and completely as Miss Quarterberry's.

"Will you hear me, child?"

Junie sighed, but answered finally, "Yes," as if jumping off a cliff for an afternoon's entertainment.

"You can see my garden," said Miss Quarterberry, forcing Junie to look into her eyes. Junie saw a mute appeal in their grey-green depths. She did not look away.

"Can you enter it?"

And Junie closed her eyes, groaned as if she had been beaten with fists, and turned her face away into the corner of the couch.

9

The Making of the Garden

"Candy floss?" said the voice.

"Why not?" said the other voice. "Add blue sky drops and a healthy root or two and it will make an admirable flower."

"And taste good, too." Laughter.

"Here, help me spread out this carpet." This after a pause and grunts of someone struggling with something heavy.

"For the lawns? Yellow grass?"

"It only needs a little water. Here." A sound of liquid being poured. "Ooops."

"Ooops? What have you done?"

"I'm afraid it wasn't water after all." Sounds of muffled laughter. "It was red wine. Do you mind the odd peony in the lawn?"

"They will be 'odd' peonies, no doubt. Look."

"Uh, oh."

"A new hybrid. The famous grape-vine peony."

"Never mind. I'll peel the grapes for you and feed them to you one by one."

"Hmph." This now unmistakably Miss Quarterberry's voice. "Feed me, indeed. Just watch what you pour onto my yellow lawn from now on."

Junie was reading. Huddled up under her covers in bed, propped on pillows in a pre-dawn greyness of light that seeped through her window, she was reading the strangest book in all the world. She could scarcely call it reading, in fact, for this book had no such details as words printed on its pages which your eyes followed left to right, top to bottom.

Sometimes voices came up from its pages and spoke to one another, making her feel as if she was eavesdropping on a conversation she really ought not to hear at all. She might shut the book quickly with a dull thud, and then cautiously open it again at another place and see pictures, this time, silent coloured pictures that did not speak, but moved, and were alive, and seemed to rise up from the pages of the book and envelop her in themselves, drawing her down into the book as into a pool of water. She would look up and gaze about her room bewildered, unsure which was more real, the bed she sat in or the book she held in her hands.

Miss Quarterberry had handed her this book when she last left the small secret room. She had in fact required her to sign it out as if it were a regular book from a regular library. When Junie protested, albeit rather meekly, that she did not have her library card with her, Miss Quarterberry had said, "What, then, is in your pocket, child? Surely you are too young to hold a credit card or a driving licence?"

And Junie, feeling about in the pocket of her jeans, had indeed found a library card there. It was the same size and shape as her own library card, but where her name usually was, were typed the words "Juniper Tree" in the unmistakable jerky script of Miss Quarterberry's typewriter. And where the name of the library ought to have been were the words "The Quarterberry Private Collection."

Miss Quarterberry produced a signing out slip and a rubber stamp from somewhere, and signed out the book. There was even a pocket on the inside back cover to hold the slip snugly in place. Peeking quickly at this, Junie saw that where the due date ought to have been stamped, were the words "Until you know your answer."

Throughout the days which had passed since then, Junie had been reading the book in all the private moments she could snatch. Gradually she began to realize that the book told a story. It told the tale of Miss Quarterberry's garden and how the garden was made. Junie found that it didn't really matter where she opened the book, for she never came across the same thing twice, and though she read it in no order or sequence of pages, turning from front to back, still the tale unfolded for her smoothly and beautifully, and all the voices and all the pictures fit together for her like two loving hands clasped together.

Once, in one of the living images the book offered up to her wondering eyes, Junie saw a pair of hands pouring bottle after bottle of brightly coloured powders into a cauldron. All the bottles were clear glass, and they held such vivid, crystalline specks of beauty that they might have held the sparkles on a lake at sunrise rather than bits of solid matter. Red and yellow, purple, aquamarine, orange, colour after colour flowed into the black depths in a series of small bright waterfalls from the glass bottles. Then a singing voice began as the liquid in the cauldron was stirred, a voice singing a song so lovely and light-hearted that Junie laughed as it sang.

And then, as the song slowed and became low and joyous and quiet, up from the cauldron rose a crowd of butterflies, all colours of the rainbow. Junie gasped in delight as she recognized them for the butterflies she had herself seen in the garden, and watched entranced as they circled and fluttered, butted one another gently and danced in their crazy circles. Caught in a shaft of sunlight like a ladder, they flew along it in a shining stream and disappeared through an upper window into the outer air.

"What about a lake?" said one of the voices when Junie opened the book. "We must have a lake, you know."

"Hmmm," said the other voice thoughtfully. "Yes. I know, take this mirror."

"Ah, perfect. And all this silly gold trim around its edges. Terribly bad taste, but it will make rather good weeds and bushes on the shore." The voice was a teasing, low man's voice.

"Bad taste, you say?" returned Miss Quarterberry's

voice, but Miss Quarterberry's voice with an extra level of richness and variety that Junie could not define. "I'll have you know it belonged to my grandmother. Give it back, if that's what you think of it."

"No, no, I've become rather fond of it after all, these past few moments."

"Return my mirror, if you please."

"Too late," said the man regretfully. "The dastardly deed is done." And Junie heard, rising up from the pages of the book, a sound of water lapping on a shore. She even caught a scent of lake water and reeds for a brief moment, before the book fell silent again in her hands, its voices fading away from her as dreams fade away from the dreamer in the harsh morning sunlight.

For all the bright images that flashed before her, Junie never once saw a face. She heard and recognized Miss Quarterberry's voice, and the unknown man's voice, in the long series of conversations they carried on together in the pages of the magical book. But though she saw hands, and powders and potions, and the garden taking shape surely out of the most unlikely ingredients, she never once saw a human face on the page opened before her.

She did not notice this at first, too interested in what was there to notice what wasn't. But once, she watched a pair of long white hands mixing some potion, moving swiftly in and out of the picture, carrying bottles and jars, turning the pages of an ancient book, stirring, and moving in strange fluttering motions over the cauldron. She knew these hands to be Miss Quarterberry's. They wore rings on their fingers, delicate gold and silver things that seemed like blossoms, growing there naturally. One wrist was circled with a thin band of gold. But beyond these strange yet familiar hands, and a glimpse of white forearms, Junie could see nothing of the person to whom they belonged.

And all at once she realized what she had been missing in the marvellous book, and even tried to peer beyond the edges of the page as one will peer sideways into a mirror as if there were a room beyond its shining reflective surface. And then she turned the pages back and forth quickly, as if they might complete the partial picture for her. They didn't, of course, and when she tried she couldn't even find the page where she had begun.

"I didn't even find out what she was making," she complained to herself, and shut the book up again with tears of frustration in her eyes. For she knew that never, never would she find that particular page again. The book offered no second chances.

She saw the hands again, though, on other pages, in other scenes. Once, free of rings, they were shaping and moulding something out of plasticine. At least, it looked more like plasticine than anything else Junie could imagine. Carefully, slowly they worked, pressing, shaping, pausing thoughtfully every now and then. Several small sculptures or shapes emerged, finally, from the large green shapeless lump with which the hands were working. Junie stared at the shapes perplexed, as they were set neatly in a row on a table.

One was a cone shape, one merely a round ball, one

was a small bear the same size as both the cone and the ball. All of them gleamed greenly from their recent contact with the warm white fingers that made them. Finally, the large green lump was entirely used up and the hands rested, one on top of the other, on the table before them. And the picture froze into stillness before Junie's eyes, and began to fade.

She turned the page quickly, hoping to discover the purpose of these strange toys. But there was no picture on the next page, only voices rising up in a conversation already begun.

" . . . been making our topiary!" exclaimed the man's voice, and Junie's ears pricked up at the familiar, recently learned word. Of course, she thought. I should have known.

"Do you like it?" asked Miss Quarterberry's voice.

"Marvellous," returned the man's voice enthusiastically. "Perfect! Not too much detail. All simple, elegant, whimsical. And will they hold their shapes, once transformed, without trimming?"

"Lazy!" scolded Miss Quarterberry, but without any real anger. "You just don't want to have to trim them yourself!"

"Quite right!" acknowledged the man. "Would you? Surely we'll have better things to do. And we can scarcely hire a gardener, can we?"

Miss Quarterberry laughed. "I suppose not. How could we explain that the bushes must be pressed back into shape rather than cut with shears? But to answer your question, yes. Yes, I believe they will hold their shape, so long as we bind some words to that effect into the final spell."

"It will be a true topiary tree, that one," said the man thoughtfully. "Holding not merely its own shape, but the form of the whole garden as well. Can it manage the task, do you think?"

"I believe so. It has strength sufficient."

Junie was sure she hadn't seen a small plasticine tree in the row on the table. What did they mean, a true topiary tree? She closed the book bewildered.

She knew she couldn't ask questions, not about the book. All she might discover about the garden, she must discover there, and from no other source.

One day, in the many days that passed while she was reading the book, she had rushed off to the library to find Miss Quarterberry and ask her about one of the spells. She was overcome with curiosity about what they used to make the rose petals. Bits of pink silk? Creamy smooth white paper cut into shapes? And how did they make them smell like roses, she wanted to know. She had seen the roses appear one day on a bright sunny page of the book, springing up on the borders of the lawn (now mysteriously but absolutely grass-green). The bushes grew swiftly, becoming full-grown in a matter of moments, and covered with lush blossoms. Delighted, she had touched the page with her finger and immediately brought forth a scent of roses, sweet and intoxicating as raspberries.

But at the library she was forestalled, once again, by the strange crowd of bespectacled adults who milled about noisily among the books. She glimpsed pink-haired Agnes and her blue-haired friend among them.

She stood gazing at them, smiling ruefully to herself, as she realized they must be Miss Quarterberry's cohorts, brought in specifically, by magical means, to prevent her from getting anywhere near Miss Quarterberry herself.

This time they all took up a rousing rendition of "Row, row, row your boat," until Junie was forced to cover her ears with her hands and move away from the noise. She knew then that she would not be able to see Miss Quarterberry until she had finished reading the book, and she walked away from the rabble disappointed.

So Junie went home again to the book, determined to get as much information as she could from it, and save questions till later. Some of her questions she wrote down in her own book, so she wouldn't forget them when she was granted an interview with Miss Quarterberry. She asked about the rose petals, the butterfly powders, how they got the lawn green, and a dozen other things until an entire page was filled with unanswered queries. Question marks ran down its right edge like so many little inky flowers.

But the book was coming to an end. Junie knew this not because she was nearing the end of its pages (still she opened the book at random), but because she could see the garden was nearly finished. Already it looked very much like the picture in the secret hall of pictures, like the garden she had seen through the windows of Miss Quarterberry's house. The hands and the voices were now concerned with details, finishing touches. They placed garden seats here and there, drew moss up through the cracks in the pathways, added a bed or two of flowers in forgotten corners. The topiary, now life-size or larger, bristled darkly in its allotted part of the garden. Junie saw a movement of birds from deep within its dense branches, and could not for a moment believe that it was made entirely of plasticine. As each thing was placed in the garden, topiary hedge, or rosebush, lawn or pool or flower bed, no matter what its source or original material, it became real. It grew and took on life, flowered or flew or sang or rippled.

It was all, so far as Junie could tell, indistinguishable from any real garden she had ever seen, except perhaps in being more beautiful, more vivid and colourful and inviting. And her new understanding of how it all came to be made cast an enchanted glow over it for her. She felt she had been let in on its secret, and so shared the garden with these two strange sorcerers who had made it.

Both pairs of hands, the man's and the woman's, carried the small tree gently, to a hole which had been dug for it. Watching, Junie knew somehow that this was a real tree, a tree like anyone might have in a garden. It was no concoction made of paper and twine or plasticine. It was real, with roots and branches, looking a little bedraggled and sorry for itself just now, but alive. The hands slowly lowered it into the hole and pressed earth around its roots, and then watered it, let the water soak into the soil, and watered it again. The little tree shivered in a passing breeze, but on the whole looked as if it had sprouted in the enchanted garden and grown there all its life.

The man's hand took hold of the woman's and both paused before the tree. There were no voices rising from this page, so Junie could not tell what words they might be saying, if any. They stood so for a long time before the little evergreen.

Finally the man moved. His hand reached down to the fresh soil at the base of the tree and picked up something that was lying there. Was it lying there all the while? Or had he just caused it to appear? Junie couldn't tell.

He held it in one hand and brushed the soil off it with the other, then held it out to the woman. Junie saw to her surprise a circle, a smallish disc like a coin, iridescent blue and green. For a brief instant she saw it whole, complete, and then the man's hands grasped it and broke it firmly in two. One half, jagged now along its broken edge, he gave to the woman. The other half he kept to himself.

"My symbol," breathed Junie. "There is another half after all." The image on the page was gone.

It felt like the end. Junie stared at the blank page before her, afraid to close the book this time for fear it would be the last time, for fear she would never be able to open it again. Was it the end? The garden was finished now, surely. But it was such a solemn, silent scene on the page which had just emptied before her. She felt there ought to be a celebration, the man's hands and Miss Quarterberry's clasping in a dance or a festival, fireworks over the garden, fresh fruits on a linen cloth on the lawn.

Junie closed the book.

But there was more. The next day when Junie retrieved the book from its hiding place, she was half afraid to open it, for fear all the pages would be blank. But she did open it, finally, and only later wished she hadn't.

For she opened it onto a storm in the garden. Snow flew across the image on the page so that Junie could barely tell it was the garden she was seeing, at first. Wind was howling and lashing the trees in a fury, pelting them with snow and hail. The flower beds and the lawns were covered with snow in drifts, ice glazed the surface of the paths, the lake was frozen. The wind blew wildly, crazily, seeming to come from all directions at once.

Junie saw with a horrible pain a butterfly struggling feebly in a drift of snow, its wings freezing in the icy wind. She turned her face away, shuddering. But the book forced her to look again. She saw the real tree now, no longer small but grown to a great height, bending and groaning in the wind. And behind and beyond the relentless voice of the wind she heard another voice, a human voice, crying in a wail of anguish. It was the man.

"Where's Miss Quarterberry?" Junie said aloud to the book, to the man, as if he could hear her. "Where is she?" Why wasn't she there, to stop the storm and the terrifying cries of the man, who sounded as if he were dying a slow, centuries-long death, dying as the garden died, in a fearful creeping merciless cold of snow and wind.

As the wind and the crying voice alike reached their highest pitch, the tree fell. It came down in a slow-motion fall before Junie's horrified eyes and landed softly, silently, on the deep snow.

Junie slammed the book shut before the image could fade and flung it violently away from her across the room.

10

Stormy Weather

The book lay where it had fallen, leaning awkwardly on the floor in a corner of Junie's room. She swore to herself that she wanted no more to do with it. She wanted no more magic gardens, no more Miss Quarterberry, no more books that betrayed you with horror after seducing you with beauty. The shining symbol she took from beneath her pillow and shoved unceremoniously into the back of a drawer. She had even tried to break it as it had once been broken before, holding it in her hands and trying with all the force she could muster to snap it in two once again. But she had not the strength, and the already broken thing would not be broken again.

She avoided the library, and even avoided reading at home, careful not to come into accidental contact with any tale of magic. She spent a great deal of time now with her mother, comforted by her coffee cups and ashtrays, and with Marcus and Victoria. She played tag with them vigorously, desperately, running madly through the long summer days, always making sure to be so very exhausted by bedtime that she left no space for uncomfortable thoughts to creep into her mind before she fell asleep.

She turned her back. She covered her ears and closed her eyes. Even her own notebook, up to now so necessary to her as a sort of private place, all her own — this too she shut up inside a drawer and would not open. For "Juniper Tree" was still written there like a threat or a reproach, and her page of questions about the garden, and these she could no longer bear to look upon. This stung the most, the sense that even her own book had been taken away from her, stolen from her like a part of herself, spoiled, ruined. And all by Miss Quarterberry.

But she could not rest, and somehow she gained no satisfaction or sense of release from all this running away, hiding away, and putting away. Whatever the reason, she found that for all her efforts she could never quite get away from "it all," as she thought of it to herself now. Things sprang up in front of her suddenly and she ran into them without being able to stop. If she thought she was going in a straight line, she would discover with dismay that it had been a circle all along, and like Alice on the other side of the looking-glass, she would find herself continually running up against the place where she began.

Fiona's library books were scattered about the house. There were books among them, not merely about topiary itself, but about trees and shrubs and hedges of all sorts. Leafing through one of these books one day, Junie was startled by a large colour photograph of the tree in the magic garden. She stared, only slowly realizing that of course it couldn't be the same tree, but was most certainly the same kind of tree, a tall evergreen against a blue sky.

"Mum?" she said as casually as she could. "What kind of tree is this?"

Fiona ambled across the room, still holding a book of her own in her hands and reading as she walked. She glanced over at the book Junie held and said, "There's your juniper tree!"

Junie shut the book up immediately and went outside.

Fiona was spending a great deal of time at Mrs. Hedges' house these days, to consult with her about her topiary, and she told Junie one morning that they had been invited there for dinner.

"She just called," said Fiona, drinking coffee as usual when Junie appeared for breakfast. "I'm not sure if it was Mary Elizabeth in very good spirits, or Fay being very self-contained, but anyway they'd like us to come for dinner with them."

"Me too?" asked Junie, who was sometimes excluded from adult gatherings.

"Yes, you too."

"Who do you think she'll be by the time we get there?" Junie asked next, always interested in the various incarnations of Mrs. Hedges.

"I don't know," said Fiona speculatively. "I suppose it would be best if Mary Elizabeth cooked, Samantha made the martinis, Fay set the table, and Alice came as a guest" — Junie was laughing now — "but we'll just have to wait and see, won't we?"

Junie was picturing Mrs. Hedges madly changing clothes every five minutes in the bathroom, like some hyperactive female Superman, and wondering what would happen if she forgot herself, and let Mary Elizabeth smoke a cigarette, for instance, or Fay fix a toilet. She might sort of come all unravelled, like an old sweater, thought Junie, and reveal the true Mrs. Hedges underneath. If there was one.

It was Mr. Hedges who opened the door to Junie and Fiona that evening when they presented themselves politely at the Hedges' front door in the cool summer twilight. He was wearing a ruffled flowery apron over his clothes and carrying a long-handled wooden spoon stained a deep orange with tomato sauce.

"I hope you like Italian," he said cheerfully, foregoing conventional greetings, and then ushered them into the house. In a moment they were instructed to join Mrs. Hedges outside in the Circus. They found her crouching beside the swings holding a screwdriver and a small oil can like the Tin Man's in *The Wizard of Oz*.

"Well, hi!" she called out heartily when she saw Junie and Fiona walking towards her across the grass. She straightened up and wiped her hands on her overalls, grinning broadly. It's Alice, thought Junie happily. Today she's Alice.

"I've just been tightening and oiling these swings," said Alice when Junie and Fiona reached her. "Can't have

Mrs. Battle hearing any suspicious creaks and squeaks from outside." And she chuckled to herself quietly, a low, "Heh, heh," that included her guests, made them co-conspirators in the protection of the Circus from intruders. Her chuckle was infectious, and Junie and Fiona were soon caught up in it too. All three of them stood there going, "Heh, heh, heh" over the well-oiled swings for a while, until Alice stopped abruptly and said, "Want a beer?"

"Sure," said Fiona, and Alice clomped back towards the house.

Mrs. Hedges returned with two bottles of beer and one of ginger ale, all clustered together between her hands. She had no glasses, but one by one she held each bottle up and flipped off its cap between her back teeth. Fiona winced slightly, watching this performance, but Junie was enthralled.

"Don't even think about it," muttered Fiona in Junie's direction.

Alice wiped off the top of the bottles on her shirt sleeve before offering them to her guests. She pulled up chairs for them to sit on, but could not sit down herself before emptying her back pockets of hammer, wrench, a handful of screws, a tape measure, and several rubber washers. Junie and Fiona watched with interest as Alice relieved herself of all this excess hardware, and Junie for one tried to figure out how it was that Alice seemed so much plumper and rounder than Fay, even though they were both the same woman.

She began to look for pillows concealed in Alice's overalls that might account for the extra padding, until

Fiona elbowed her and whispered, "Don't stare!"

Junie gave her an aggrieved look, for surely she had been staring too, and then began to gaze pointedly around the Circus.

Alice and Fiona were speaking in quiet voices about the repair of the fountain, which wasn't working properly. Alice seemed quite pleased about the prospect of fixing it. "It's Harold, you know," she was confiding to Fiona. "He can't stand it when the fountain's out. Or when the swings squeak, or the golf course creaks. Everything has to be shipshape, just so, rigged and ready, swabbed and scrubbed." And Alice gazed around the Circus, its colours subdued in the fading light, as if it were indeed a ship waiting at anchor, and needing only a few minor adjustments under Alice's skilful hands before setting sail triumphantly down the street, astonishing Mrs. Battle, the neighbourhood, the town, the world.

Junie and Fiona looked around, too, as if it were expected of them. Fiona made some small murmurs of appreciation, but Junie was gazing at the tall hedges surrounding the Circus, thinking.

"Maybe," she said thoughtfully, "maybe you could mould those hedges into sails, like on a sailing ship, and then you really could sail away!"

"Mould?" said Fiona laughing. "She talks as if they were made of clay!" she added to Mrs. Hedges.

Junie reddened and fell silent. She had been thinking of the topiary in Miss Quarterberry's magic garden in spite of herself. She had almost imagined her mother up on a ladder with a trowel rather than pruning shears, pressing the hedges into the proper shape rather than trimming them. Remembering the magic garden at this moment cast her into gloom again, and she remained silent.

"Well now, sails!" said Mrs. Hedges kindly, surveying the borders of her kingdom as if she too were trying to picture green, leafy sails billowing proudly over its treasures. "Mould is a good word, too, you know," she went on, tapping her hammer on one palm. "It's sort of like sculptuary, or statuary, or whatever-ary, this topiary, isn't it?"

"Sure is," said Fiona, sighing as if for a moment she regretted what she'd taken on, in promising to sculpt the Hedges' hedges for them.

"Is it hard, Mum?" asked Junie, suddenly realizing she had no notion of how topiary shapes were usually made, in the ordinary unmagical world.

"Well, it's slow," said Fiona. "You have to be very patient and careful, and remember the trees are living things while you're working with them. And then, it's getting them to hold their shapes that's the tricky part. You wouldn't want a topiary bird to grow an extra few wings, for instance, or a bear to have ten leafy ears."

"No, I guess not," said Junie unhappily. Hold their shapes, she thought. Topiary everywhere. She frowned down at her ginger ale bottle, thinking about the mysterious man in the book, the man saying, "It must hold not merely its own shape, but the form of the whole garden as well." What was he talking about? How could one topiary tree hold a whole garden together? Why did it need to be held together? "Oh who cares," muttered Junie angrily under her breath, furious to find herself thinking about the garden again.

She was startled out of her reverie by the sound of a low, loud gong from inside the house, signalling dinner.

"Now what I would like to know," said Alice to Fiona as they all trooped into the house, "is this: can you do one in the shape of a wrench?"

On the Hedges' big dining room table, Harold had set out bowl after bowl of steaming food, and he stood beaming over it all as his guests came in.

"My goodness!" exclaimed Fiona at the sight of the feast waiting before them, and Mr. Hedges beamed a little brighter.

"*Linguine, fettucine, tortellini,*" he chanted happily as they all sat down, gesturing at one bowl after another. "*Pasta, antipasto, pesto.*" And then, brimming over with excitement and pleasure in his culinary skill, he burst into song, bustling around with wine glasses and napkins and doing a little dance as he sang.

"Sit down and eat," protested Alice. "It all looks delicious."

And Harold sat down, lifting his glass to his wife and his guests in turn, saying, "*Bon appetit!*"

"*Macaroni,*" responded Alice, lifting her own glass back to him.

"Cheese," said Fiona.

"No swearing at the table," reproved Mr. Hedges, pretending to frown sternly at her from under his eyebrows. But Alice and Junie were laughing so hard that soon he too collapsed back in his chair and mopped the frown off his face with his handkerchief.

It began to rain outside as they ate, and through the dining room window Junie could see the lightning flashing in eerie patterns across the dark sky. Mr. and Mrs. Hedges and her mother didn't even pause in their eager talking and eating as the storm blew in, but Junie stopped eating to look from the sky ouside to the bright warm table inside, lit with orange candles which shone on the happy faces all around her.

There was a pause then, and all four faces looked up as a loud thunderclap interrupted the conversation. The candles flickered.

"Don't know why . . . " began Fiona in a very quiet voice.

"Ain't no sun up in the sky . . . " continued Mrs. Hedges, singing around a mouthful and trying not to laugh.

"Stormy weather!" sang Mr. Hedges loudly and dramatically, rising up out of his seat as if he were on a stage. And in a moment he and Alice were both up together, dancing in one another's arms around the table, keeping time to Harold's crooning as the storm raged outside the window.

In the candlelight Junie watched Alice's overalls turning and turning in the arms of Mr. Hedges' dinner jacket as the two danced, moving as gracefully around the table as if they were in a ballroom, and she wanted all at once to laugh and to cry at the sight of them.

But after ice-cream, for Junie, and coffee, for Fiona, and yawns of sleepiness, and the walk home after the rain in the fresh, moist night air, Junie found herself wide awake in bed, staring at the ceiling.

She gave in.

She felt her way over to where the magic book lay on the floor and picked it up gently, smoothing its covers with her fingers as if it were a small, lonely animal. Then she flicked on her desk light and got out her notebook. She opened it up to the page of questions she had written there about the magic garden, took a pencil, and drew a line through them all. They didn't matter now. They didn't matter at all. Through the magic book she had fallen in love with the magic garden, and it didn't matter now how the rose petals were made or how the grass became green. What mattered now was the whole garden, taken all together, shining like a dream or a vision from the pages of the book. Even the horrible storm that had blighted the charmed place, even that now seemed to Junie only another proof of the place's loveliness.

Turning to a fresh page in her book she wrote two more questions on it: "Do I want to go there?" she wrote, and, "Can I get there?" Then, taking a deep breath, she wrote the answers as well: "Yes," she wrote. And, "I think so."

11

Say the Trees Have Ears

At the breakfast table the next morning Junie sat preoccupied, toying with her toast and stirring her cereal as if it were coffee. She was trying to put things together in her mind.

Miss Quarterberry made a magic garden, that's one, she thought to herself. Two: Miss Quarterberry and a man made a magic garden. So far so good. She was trying to build it all up in her mind as if she was building a house out of blocks. She wanted to be able to see each one of the blocks, know what it was, and find out how it fit in with every other block.

Three: Miss Quarterberry and a man made a magic garden together and planted one real tree in it.

Four: Miss Quarterberry and a man made a magic garden together and planted one real tree in it — a juniper tree (and that's me, too!).

Five: but the tree fell down in the storm. She frowned and shuddered even at the thought of the storm, but took hold of herself and went on.

Six: Miss Quarterberry wants me to go into the garden.

Oh, darn. Five and a half: now Miss Quarterberry can't even see the garden any more.

And, five and three-quarters: there's a horrible old man in the garden now, who might be the one who made it so she can't even see the garden any more. Junie paused here, considering the frightful portrait of the man, and wondering who he was, and why Miss Quarterberry kept a picture of him.

OK, now six: Miss Quarterberry wants me to go into the garden.

As she put five and three-quarters next to six, she gulped. She had almost forgotten about the frightening old man, and yet Miss Quarterberry said he was there. And she was supposed to go in there, where he was? A long finger of fear crept into her belly as she sat, and she pushed away the remains of her breakfast.

Yesterday I thought I wanted to go there, she said to herself, and sighed longingly at the thought of the mar-vellous place. But if that man is there ... do I? The blocks weren't fitting together at all, and she stared at the table in front of her as if it was littered with real blocks of all shapes and sizes, blocks that wouldn't make a house for her despite all her efforts.

But all at once a new question entered her mind. Why does she want me to go there? Why?

Junie stood at the door of Number 13 Mulberry Street clutching the magic book to her side. She shifted from one foot to the other, then took hold of the symbol, which she had retrieved from her drawer and now held inside her pocket. It felt solid and reassuring to her touch, and seemed to give her the courage she needed. She let it go and knocked firmly on the door, once, twice.

The door opened slowly. In front of her stood Agnes, wearing the maid's outfit with the cap and the apron.

"Yes?" said Agnes, looking Junie up and down.

"Hi," said Junie, gazing at Agnes imploringly, willing her to remember who she was. "I have a book to return to Miss Quarterberry. Don't you remember me? It's me — Juniper Tree."

Agnes's face softened as Junie said these words, and she smiled suddenly, as if Junie had just come into focus for her.

"Oh, of course," she said apologetically. "Please come in, Juniper Tree."

Junie watched with bewilderment as Agnes seemed to transform before her very eyes, becoming the sprightly old lady of the library instead of the stiff maid.

"Read any good books lately?" said Agnes confidingly, and then laid one forefinger along the side of her nose and nodded.

"Well, yes, I guess so," said Junie, glancing down at the magic book.

Agnes laughed and clapped her hands at this answer, crying, "That's right! Good for you!" And then she hurried out of the room, saying, "In a moment! In a moment!" as if Junie had demanded something of her immediately, and chuckled off down the hallway.

But she returned almost at once, saying, "Well, hurry up! Come along!" and once again led Junie through the labyrinth of Miss Quarterberry's house. At the door to the library, she said, "In you go! Never fear! Read any good books lately?" and then sped off down the corridor as if she had wheels under her instead of feet.

So Junie stood up very tall in front of the doorway, cheered by Agnes's cryptic encouragement, and threw the door open. Miss Quarterberry was sitting at the long table with a book open before her, and she looked up as Junie made her grand entrance.

"Don't say a word," Junie announced, holding up one hand. "I have just a few questions," she said, pacing up and down the floor and becoming more Sherlock Holmes every moment. "Just one or two small questions before I tell you my — conclusion." She glanced sidelong at Miss Quarterberry, expecting to see disapproval on her face. But Miss Quarterberry merely sat back with her arms folded, looking seriously at Junie. She said, simply, "Very well."

"Oh." Junie was disconcerted at the lack of opposition, and found all at once that she couldn't carry on the charade any longer. She sat down heavily in a chair opposite Miss Quarterberry. Glancing over at the window, she saw the curtains were drawn together, preventing her getting even a glimpse of the garden. She looked down at the book in her hands, and wondered at it, at the way it held the garden inside itself, folded up and put away like an old letter. And for a moment she thought that all she needed to do was open the window and step through it to enter the magic garden. It might be that easy, that effortless, like slipping into a pool of water or opening her eyes in the morning.

When Junie had neglected to begin her promised questioning Miss Quarterberry had turned back to her book. She sat now, very calm and straight in her chair, gazing down at the book in front of her as if she had forgotten Junie was there.

"What are you reading?" Junie asked quietly.

"Nineteenth-century sermons, actually," Miss Quarterberry replied, and then shut up the book with a snap. "Is that what you came to ask me?"

"No." Junie was at a loss. "Oh, aren't you going to help me at all?" she complained, a whine creeping into her voice.

"When did you ask for my help?" returned Miss Quarterberry. "Shall I take your arm and lead you across the street? Do your homework for you? Escort you home?"

Junie looked at her resentfully for a moment. "Now," she said. "I'm asking now."

And Miss Quarterberry said nothing, but spread out her two long white hands before her, though whether in welcome or entreaty, Junie could not say.

"This is a wonderful book," Junie said, handing the magic book across the table to Miss Quarterberry.

Miss Quarterberry opened the book, took out the check-out slip and peered disapprovingly at it. "Not overdue," she sighed as if she was disappointed, and then blew on the slip of paper in her hand, and it vanished.

"You said you wanted me to go into that garden," Junie went on, stifling an urge to ask about the trick.

"I asked if you were able to do so," corrected Miss Quarterberry. "But, as it happens, I have also a desire that you should."

"Why?"

"Why did I ask you?"

"No, why do you want me to go there?"

Miss Quarterberry looked at her, genuinely surprised. "You don't know?" she asked unbelievingly. "Why, if you go, Juniper Tree, I may be able to follow."

Junie sat back in her chair. "But if you made it, and everything . . . " she paused. "I thought you could do anything. Why can't you just go there any old time you want?"

Miss Quarterberry shook her head. "I cannot. I have lost the way." She spoke as if she had misplaced the way into the garden like a set of keys or a necklace.

"I cannot so much as see its leaves shifting in a dawn wind, Juniper Tree, or the dew on the grass, or the play of its shadows in the evening. How should I be able to go there, when," and she laughed a little, ruefully, "when I do not even know, any more, where it is?"

"But it's your garden, Miss Quarterberry!" Junie protested. "You made it. Why can't you get to it?"

"I left it," Miss Quarterberry answered. "I left it, once, and once I left it, I could not return."

"Why, Miss Quarterberry? Why did you leave?"

"That, child, is none of your affair." Junie felt as if she had been slapped. And she felt, to her dismay, a prickling of painful tears behind her eyes. Oh, what am I doing here? she thought. Who is this Miss Quarterberry anyway? She's not even nice to me! And she almost, in her anger and pain, got up and left there and then. "My mother says I shouldn't talk to strangers," she would say as she left, very calmly and with dignity. That would get her.

Just as the muscles in the back of her legs began to tighten, to lift her out of the chair and carry her away from Miss Quarterberry, she looked up and saw Miss Quarterberry herself standing up, wringing her hands in agitation.

"Listen to me, Juniper Tree," she said urgently, and Junie realized with a shock that she was suffering, suffering too much and too deeply to notice Junie's petulance.

"Say the trees have ears," she said, speaking to Junie but also seeming to implore the books around her, the table and chairs, the air itself. "Say they have heard all the murmurs down the centuries that we have missed, or thought we heard, but misheard. Say the trees have ears, and not only ears but voices too. They might have heard things spoken under their boughs a hundred years ago, or in another place and time, words of love or passion or hate or pain. They might be able to tell those words to us, make the old times real for us, make them come again in the telling. Say the trees have ears, Juniper Tree. Do you? Are you listening?"

Junie nodded, trying to understand.

"I will try to explain what cannot be explained," continued Miss Quarterberry more slowly, seeing Junie's face. She took a deep breath as if trying to gather her thoughts. "You have read the book?" she asked.

Again Junie nodded.

"Very well. You know, then, about the making of the garden. And truly enough you deserve to know more, after what I have asked of you." She paused and looked apologetically at Junie. "Forgive me, child, for expecting too much of you, for asking you to dive into an unknown sea. I have been reluctant to tell you more of my story because it is a very private thing, a tale told in the quiet places of my heart, in a secret language."

Junie sat very still now, waiting, and watching the tall, plain woman before her who seemed to be so many different women. Junie watched, and believed in all those women as surely as she believed in the angles of Miss Quarterberry's face when it was turned away from her.

"There are some things difficult to tell, Juniper Tree, not because they are complicated but because they are private. I will try to tell you my story, try to tell you why I ask you to go into my garden, but I am afraid I cannot fully explain why it is painful in the telling.

"Another person and I made a garden," she began, unconsciously echoing the shape of Junie's own thoughts earlier in the day. "We made it for pleasure, for our own pleasure, for privacy, for the delight of using the power in our fingertips. You saw how we made it."

Junie nodded again, remembering.

"You saw, then, that it was made by magic, by a judicious yet also playful combining of ingredients, spells, and the power of transforming that lies here." She held one long white hand to her breast.

"Magic is fragile," she continued when she saw Junie was following her. "I know this may sound strange, Juniper

Tree, but it is both strong and easily broken. Like an egg. Think of eggs." Junie dutifully thought of eggs, and saw a plate before her with toast and two fried eggs on it.

"No, no," said Miss Quarterberry, once again as if she could read Junie's mind. "An egg." And all at once Miss Quarterberry was holding an ordinary chicken's egg up before Junie.

"Behold the egg," she said, and then she was a magician of the sort who pulls rabbits out of hats. She was wearing a top hat, a formal long-tailed man's coat, trousers and shoes with white spats, still holding the egg in one hand, and a long silver-tipped cane in the other.

"Behold the egg," she repeated in a stagey sort of way, delicately touching the silvered end of the cane to the egg's white shell. "A lovely thing, is it not? No hidden doors, you will observe, no hinges, no tricks of any kind." Junie shook her head earnestly.

"Very well," said Miss Quarterberry. "The egg. Like a ball, it can be juggled." And all at once there were many eggs, all flying in the air as Miss Quarterberry juggled them. They made a swift white ring moving above her head, and she moved back and forth underneath them, concentrating on one spot in the air above her head as her hands unerringly caught and tossed, caught and tossed.

Junie was just about to clap in delight at the performance when all the eggs but one vanished. This last egg Miss Quarterberry caught neatly in one hand. Then she tossed the egg to Junie, who very nearly missed catching it. But Miss Quarterberry, smiling, gestured to Junie to toss it back to her.

"Ah, the egg," said Miss Quarterberry, holding it once

again between thumb and forefinger. "So very like a ball, is it not? One can juggle it, one can play catch with it, one can put it safely away . . . " And here she took off her top hat, dropped the egg into it, and put the hat back on her head, tapped it down with her cane and, to Junie's astonishment, turned several cartwheels across the room. She stood upright again, took off the hat, and lifted out the egg from within it, saying, " . . . and take it out again, unharmed." And Junie was invited to inspect the egg again.

"So very like a ball," Miss Quarterberry repeated with a flourish, "except in one tiny particular." She held the egg up dramatically. Junie held her breath.

"The egg . . . " Miss Quarterberry paused, looked at the egg, and shrugged. She let it go, and Junie heard with a wince the very small crack and splatter it made as it smashed to bits on the floor. " . . . simply will not bounce."

Junie had leaned sideways to look under the table, trying to see the broken egg. But the floor was smooth and clean wherever she looked, and when she sat upright again Miss Quarterberry was once again Miss Quarterberry. The magician's outfit had vanished, and one long hand was patting a stray hair into place on the neat head. Junie sighed, sorry the magic show was over so quickly. But she knew, too, that she was here for something much more important than a magic show, and she waited expectantly for what might come next.

"Magic is fragile," Miss Quarterberry repeated. "Like eggs."

Junie smiled a slow, sad smile, thinking not only of the broken egg, but of the broken symbol which she held yet in her pocket. She fingered its hard smoothness gently.

"The magic that made our garden, Juniper Tree, is as fragile as all magic. It needs vigilance and care to protect it, to keep it whole."

"Like real gardens, too?" ventured Junie, thinking of her mother's round of pruning, weeding, mowing, and trimming.

"Yes," said Miss Quarterberry kindly. "Yes, like real gardens too, child. But this garden needs a different sort of care. No weeds grow there, except the ones we chose. The grass does not need mowing, the topiary needs no trimming. The garden was a place built for pleasure, not for work. But — in order to hold it all together, to keep it blooming, to keep the grass from fading back into a carpet again, the dandelions melting into lemon-drops, the lake stiffening into a mirror, we needed to make a spell very strong indeed, a spell woven into something that had the strength to hold it."

"It's all like Cinderella," said Junie dreamily. "Like the pumpkin coach, and the lizard footmen."

"Yes, and what happened to the coach at midnight?" asked Miss Quarterberry.

"It turned back into a pumpkin."

"Precisely. Similar spell," said Miss Quarterberry.

"Oh — " Junie made the connection. "So you mean your garden, at midnight, would all turn back into what you made it from?"

"Not for many, many midnights," corrected Miss Quarterberry. "Our spells were much stronger than those," she preened herself smugly. "But then — fairy godmothers always were rather a feeble breed." She snorted contemptuously. "But eventually, Juniper Tree, yes, the garden would have begun to decay, or been discovered, for the final spell also protected it from the outside, set it beyond the illusions of space and time which so hinder this world.

"So, as the book has its cover, to keep the words from flying off in all directions, and the picture its frame, to hold it on the wall, so likewise our garden needed something — solid — something real, something untouched by magic, something strong and true as steel — to protect it, to keep it whole."

Junie had a sinking feeling inside. She began to slump down in the chair. But it was no good. She didn't have time to slide completely underneath the table before Miss Quarterberry came and stood opposite her, placed her two hands flat on the table and leaned towards her.

"You know what we did, don't you, Juniper Tree?" she said, very gently.

Junie shook her head, but stayed silent.

"Come now, child," persisted Miss Quarterberry, still in the same gentle voice. "You have read the book."

"So?" said Junie rudely.

Miss Quarterberry straightened, irritation clouding her face. She took a step or two away from Junie, saying, "Not only is it very foolish to pretend ignorance when you have knowledge, child, it is also despicable. It is not — " she whirled around angrily. "It is not honourable, Juniper Tree. It is beneath you to stoop to such tactics."

Junie wished, hearing these words, that she could

crawl underneath the table and hide there forever. She looked down, avoiding Miss Quarterberry's eyes. A painful mixture of fear and shame churned in her belly.

From the corner of her eye she saw the pair of long white hands clenched together, pulling and wringing. But Miss Quarterberry said not a word, and Junie was forced to endure the silence and the tumult of her own thoughts, until she felt she could bear them no longer.

"You planted a tree," she murmured under her breath.

"What kind of a tree?" Miss Quarterberry was beside her in a moment, and Junie saw, as she looked up, something in her face that she could only call relief.

"A real tree." Junie spoke more clearly now, as if in uttering the words she gained a kind of courage she did not know she had.

"Yes?"

"A juniper tree."

"A juniper tree," repeated Miss Quarterberry solemnly. "We planted a juniper tree, the one real, living thing in our garden, child. And as we planted it, we wove into it a spell, so that it would, as it grew, be the guardian and the protector of the place. And it flourished. It took root, and grew, and lived. It watched over the garden silently but surely, and it overheard all our laughter and joy when we two were there. It held all the magic of the place inside itself, and preserved it, and kept it whole."

"The trees have ears," whispered Junie.

"This tree had ears, in a way, child. I do not mean that it had ears like yours, that it nodded and answered and argued with you when you spoke to it," she said, smiling.

"I mean that in its strength and beauty and life, it heard the life of the garden, and knew it, and took care of it, just as you, child, have heard the life of the garden, and know it, because you read it in the book."

"I think I know what you mean," said Junie thoughtfully. "Like a Christmas tree seems to know it's Christmas, and make it Christmas, or the way the tree in my backyard seems to like to be climbed. But, Miss Quarterberry," Junie was troubled. "The tree fell."

"The tree fell," assented Miss Quarterberry. Her voice was serious but not desperate, and Junie felt calmer, hearing the calmness in Miss Quarterberry's tone. "Yes, child. That is the sad ending to my story."

She took a deep breath. "We quarrelled, we two. The reasons seem foolish now. I can barely recall them myself. They are unimportant, except in that we allowed them to seem important then, and quarrelled bitterly. And in my anger, I left the garden. When I left, I did not think I would never be able to return. I did not know it would be for the last time."

Miss Quarterberry looked up and saw the dismay on Junie's face. She laid her hand on Junie's arm and spoke reassuringly. "Child," she said. "It is a very sad story, but it all happened a long time ago. Here I am, you see." She held her hands out at her sides. "I survived it. Do not let it fill you with despair.

"After we quarrelled, after I left," she resumed, "he brought a storm onto the garden. You saw it." Junie nodded.

"Very well. His powers were — are — formidable, and he, like me, does not do things by halves." Junie saw that she was smiling slightly, and even spoke with a kind of affection.

"But he destroyed your garden, Miss Quarterberry!" she protested.

"Did he?" asked Miss Quarterberry. "How then should you still see it, living, blooming, outside my window?" Junie frowned. She didn't know the answer.

"He brought a storm onto the garden, venting his anger towards me on the place we had created together. And — whether it was intended or not, the storm brought down our juniper tree. It was a real tree, you see. Real trees can die.

"But this storm, like all storms, ended. And even magic gardens have a certain resilience. The tree was gone; it could not be saved. But the snow melted eventually, the garden, so you say, blooms again. Remember that I have not seen the place since then, child. I have only your word for how it has fared."

"But without the tree — " faltered Junie. She had a sudden sense of unease and uncertainty. She had seen the garden, it was true, but how could she be sure of it? Even when she had seen it, it had seemed an unlikely sort of place, appearing out of nowhere, hovering before her eyes like something seen in a dream. Perhaps it wasn't really as she had seen it — perhaps it had clicked into focus for her for a moment like a pattern seen in a kaleidoscope, never to be captured again. She had never seen the tree in it, after all, and without the tree, which she knew now to be the heart and soul of the place, could the garden really be there?

"Ah, yes. Without the tree," answered Miss Quarterberry, recalling Junie's attention. "We had, it seems, made our spell even better than we knew. When the tree fell, my way was closed into the garden. I could not get back no matter how hard, how long, how desperately I tried. And I did try." Her voice was still calm, but Junie sensed a remembered pain beneath it that filled her with pity.

"The juniper tree, I found, was more than a protector. It was the way into the place too. The only way." She paused for a long moment.

"Now you know the tale, Juniper Tree. Do you see what I am asking of you?"

"I think so," said Junie. "You want me to be like a new juniper tree for you, so that maybe you can get back into your garden again."

Miss Quarterberry nodded silently. And for the first time it occurred to Junie that if Miss Quarterberry managed to reach her garden, she would disappear forever from Junie's life, from her world. But Junie pushed this thought away. It was too difficult, too painful to think about now.

"Miss Quarterberry," she said instead, "I had a sort of a feeling inside that I could get into the garden, somehow. But I don't know the way. How do I get there?"

"I cannot tell you, child."

"But, how — "

"Listen. I cannot tell you the way, you must find it for yourself." She spoke with a sudden urgency again, as if she had been controlling it as she told her tale, but could no longer contain it now that the tale was told. "If I told you the way, Juniper Tree, it would be another concoction, a bit of magic, a spell. It might — I don't know — but it might just be possible for me to conjure you into the garden. I cannot reach it myself — my way has been closed. Nor can I give you a list of directions, because even if there were such a thing, it has been erased from my mind, swept away. You are a different matter. You — I might be able to send there somehow, as if I were firing an arrow at a place I cannot see.

"But if I did that, it would be as if I had made you up, as I made up the topiary and the rose bushes. Do you see? I would be placing you there, controlling you, making you up. It would be a kind of cheating, cheating the magic of the place. And magic cannot be deceived. It wouldn't work.

"This juniper tree was a real tree. You are a real child, linked to that one real tree we planted. I could make a doll that looked like you and send it, perhaps, into the garden. But it would not be you, for all my magic. The whole point is that you are *outside* the magic. Remember the cover of the book? The frame of the picture? You *must* find the way for yourself, if you choose to do this for me. I cannot force you to do it, you know. I can only ask you."

Junie looked up at her blankly. She had no idea how one went about getting inside a magic garden.

"I don't know if I can do it," she said finally.

"Nor do I, child. But you said you had a feeling inside that you might. Never underestimate such feelings. Trust it, follow it — it may help you find the way. And if you do truly decide to try, I would not reproach you if you failed. Even in the trying, you would bring me closer to my garden."

"OK," said Junie. "I'll do it. I'll try." She spoke with a cheerful certainty that seemed to come to her from outside, like a gift.

"Thank you, Juniper Tree," said Miss Quarterberry, clasping Junie's hands warmly. "You do not know what a great gift you are giving me. Thank you."

But Junie remembered something in that instant, the moment after she had given her promise, that almost made her regret what she had done.

"What happened to him?" she asked abruptly. "To the man?"

"Why, nothing, child," said Miss Quarterberry, as if surprised at the question.

"Nothing?" Junie's voice was rising. "Where is he, Miss Quarterberry?"

"He is still in the garden, child. Surely you knew? When the tree fell, the door closed. I could not go back, and he — he could not leave."

"But, Miss Quarterberry," protested Junie, trying to keep her voice from shaking. "You said — you said before that that man in the picture — " and here she shuddered involuntarily, remembering the face — "that old man was in the garden. Are they both there?"

"Both?" said Miss Quarterberry. "They are one, child. The portrait is of him; he is that man."

Junie swallowed, a dreadful realization coming to her. "I didn't know *he* was — " she thought of the picture. "I didn't know they were the same person. I didn't know." She looked wildly at Miss Quarterberry. "And you and him — " Junie was filled with horror.

"You and he," corrected Miss Quarterberry.

"Whatever!" shouted Junie. "You and him were, are —"

"Lovers," said Miss Quarterberry. "Yes."

"Yuk," said Junie.

"I beg your pardon?"

"Oh, Miss Quarterberry, I didn't know, I didn't know it was him." She couldn't stop repeating the same phrase, stupidly.

Miss Quarterberry gazed at her, perplexed. Then she snapped her fingers and the picture appeared in her hands. She looked at it thoughtfully.

"Not beautiful, truly, child." Junie peered sidelong at the face again, then looked away.

"But no more am I," went on Miss Quarterberry, regardless of Junie's trembling. "This is my only link to him now. It is all I have left of him. And I have watched it change, age and sicken, and I have been able to do nothing. Nothing." She continued looking at the face in the picture for a few moments, then stretched out a finger and caressed it gently, as if she were touching skin rather than paint on canvas. Junie shuddered again.

"Oh, for goodness' sake," said Miss Quarterberry in irritation. "What is so frightening?" She held the picture out to Junie. Junie forced herself to look at it. She saw again the young man's bearded face, the ancient eyes.

"It is a face marked by despair and pain, Juniper Tree," said Miss Quarterberry. "I know it is not lovely. But it may be lovelier — soon."

Junie looked at Miss Quarterberry and tried to take courage from the kindness she saw in the depths of those grey-green eyes. But then she glanced back at the picture, at the colourless eyes that gazed out at her, and she felt the long finger of fear creep into her belly again, and was certain of nothing.

12

Research

"How do you get to a place when you don't know where it is?"

"Find out where it is. Get a map."

"Oh, a map. I don't think there is one."

"No map? Where is this place, anyway?"

"That's what I'd like to know!"

"You're going to have to tell me what you're talking about if you want me to help you, you know," Marcus said.

Junie looked up at him blankly. She longed to tell somebody about Miss Quarterberry and the magic garden, but she was almost afraid to speak of it, for fear she might break the spell. She was very confused and a little frightened, but she didn't want the magic to end, not for anything. She rolled over onto her back and groaned, looking up at the sky.

"This is very boring, you know," said Marcus presently. "Watching you lying on the grass like an old log. Not exciting at all. Dull. Uninteresting." He was rolling a ball back and forth on the grass to entertain Victoria, but Victoria knew his heart wasn't in it, and she sat watching him quizzically.

Junie glanced at him. His glasses were sliding down his nose, as usual, and he looked hurt and resentful. Why, I've been horrible lately, she realized. Thinking about me and Miss Quarterberry all the time, all wrapped up in it, hardly even talking to him. No wonder he's acting so funny. I wonder, she mused. I wonder if I could?

"Marcus," she burst out. "Can you keep a secret?"

"What do you think?" he snapped back.

"I'm sorry," Junie murmured. "I'm sorry, of course you can, I know." She saw on reflection that he had the unmistakable air of a true secret-keeper. "Are you interested in keeping one for me, then?" she said.

"I guess," said Marcus, softening a little. "Tell away."

So she told. It all came pouring out in a rush, as if her voice knew better than she when it needed to be used, and she told things as they popped into her head, speaking very quickly. When she was done, she sat back, took a deep breath, and waited for Marcus to express his astonishment.

"Well," he said at last, as if someone had just given him a grocery list rather than a catalogue of marvels such as Junie had just related.

"Well? That's all you can say?" she protested.

"All for now," he replied calmly. "I have to think this over." Then he whistled for Victoria to follow him and walked away, leaving Junie sitting behind him with her secret spilled all over the grass. It was out now; it could not be gathered up again and put away. And she looked around as if she was seeing all her words scattered around her, and did not know whether to laugh or cry.

For a horrible moment she expected the worst. Either Marcus thought she was completely out of her mind, and would have nothing more to do with her, or he thought she was completely out of her mind, and would expose her. He would gather some boys, tell them her tale, and taunt her, with them, as she walked to and from school. Probably they would throw stones at her. She tried to face the fact calmly that her entire life was ruined.

But strangely, Marcus and Victoria appeared at her front door the next morning, as Junie and Fiona were having breakfast. Fiona wandered to the door with a slice of toast in her hand and invited them in. Junie heard their voices in the hallway and held her breath. "Mrs. Summers," she expected Marcus to say in a solemn tone. "I think there's something you ought to know about your daughter." She began to be a little relieved when they did not turn away into the living room to talk privately, but came instead straight back into the kitchen.

"Would you like some breakfast?" Fiona was saying to Marcus, and Victoria bounded cheerfully over to Junie at the table and licked her face.

"Yes, please," said Marcus, and sat down prepared to eat several pieces of toast with jam, a glass of juice, a glass of milk, and a cinnamon bun as if he hadn't eaten for weeks. He was carrying a large, bulgy bag with him, Junie noticed, but otherwise seemed his usual self.

"Let me do the dishes for you, Mrs. Summers," offered Marcus when he had swallowed the absolute last morsel of food he could manage.

"I'll take you up on that, Marcus," said Fiona. "I've got to dash out this morning to the Hedges'." They heard Fiona's voice calling goodbye over the splash of water and the clinking of dishes in the sink.

"Well?" said Junie, grabbing a tea-towel to help.

Marcus grinned at her, and hooted as he tossed a handful of suds into the air. "This," he said happily, "is great! Why on earth didn't you tell me before? To think it's been going on all summer, all this magic stuff — and you never let on for a minute!"

"OK, Juniper Tree," he said when they had finished the dishes and were settled again at the table. "What are we going to do first?"

Junie was a little abashed at hearing "Juniper Tree" from his lips — it sounded both foolish and also somehow important to hear someone other than Miss Quarterberry say it.

"Well, first," said Junie, all at once highly relieved and pleased to be able to discuss the matter with somebody. "I have to find a way to get into that magic garden."

"Yes, but how?" said Marcus practically. "Are you going to go to the bus station and ask how much a ticket is to never-never land, or what? We ought to go about this thing scientifically. We have to work out where to begin."

"Yeah," agreed Junie, sighing. "But I'm not really even sure how to do that."

"Hmmm," said Marcus. "Well, let's think of how we *can't* do it, first of all. Process of elimination."

"Precisely, my dear Watson," said Junie. "Not by bus, first off."

"Or by car, or train, or plane." Marcus counted off on his fingers all the conventional means of travel he could think of. "If it's a magic place," he suggested, "maybe you can only get there some magic way."

"Magic carpet," sighed Junie despondently, and then her eye fell on one of Fiona's sketchbooks. "Or — " she said, rising up from her chair and grabbing Marcus's arm, "or — seven-league boots!"

"Might as well go looking for a magic carpet," returned Marcus. "Where on earth are you going to find seven-league boots?"

"Where on earth?" said Junie. "Here!" And she rummaged through the sketchbooks until she found Fiona's latest drawing of the pair of boots. She held the page out triumphantly to Marcus.

"Remember? Even you said they could be seven-league boots."

Marcus stared at the page with distaste. "That," he said, as if speaking to a very small child, "is a picture of a pair of boots. A picture. It isn't real."

"Oh, real," said Junie impatiently, feeling he was quibbling over details. Looking at the picture, she remembered her dreams of the boots, so vivid in their exultation and fear, dreams as real as anything she knew, as real as Marcus and Victoria, she thought, as real as breakfast.

"C'mon — let's get serious," said Marcus, ignoring the picture. "We'll work out how to get there later." With one swift gesture he flipped the picture over face down on the table and laid several sketchbooks on top of it, as if to prevent those mysterious boots from getting up off the page and walking away.

"Let's think about it all differently," he said, pacing up and down the kitchen. "There's this magic garden. You've never really been in it, so you don't know where it is, exactly. But you've seen it, right?"

Reluctantly dropping the subject of the boots, since Marcus refused to consider it, Junie followed his lead. "Yes, I've seen it," she answered. "More than once. First in the picture —"

"Oh, pictures again — pshaw!" said Marcus contemptuously. He really did say "pshaw," pronouncing each letter of a word Junie had thought only ever appeared in books. She gazed at Marcus, amazed at his boldness in seizing such an awkward word and making it his own.

"Where else?" he was asking her.

"Oh, um — out of windows, two windows in Miss Quarterberry's house. But you know this is the weird thing. I saw the same view from both windows, as if the garden ran around outside the house to surprise me when I got to the next room!"

"Gardens can't run around!" said Marcus.

"No, I know," said Junie helplessly. "But that's what I saw. She said it wasn't really there."

"Wasn't really there?"

"That's what she said," protested Junie. "And you know, Marcus, she couldn't see it! Even though she made it, it was invisible to her, as if it wasn't really there."

"You're *sure* you saw it?" Marcus asked.

"Yes!" exclaimed Junie, indignant. "I could draw you a picture of it if you didn't have this weird thing about pictures!"

"OK, OK," soothed Marcus. "OK. You know what," he said, "it's like — like it's in another dimension or something, here, there, and everywhere, sort of in our world and not in it at the same time."

"Well, I know that!" snorted Junie. "It's magic!" She felt they weren't making any progress at all.

But Marcus said, "Sooo, we have to find out the best route to take to get into another dimension!"

Junie groaned and put her arms over her head.

"No, listen, listen!" said Marcus. "Remember I said you needed a map before? Well, that's what we need, a map or something to tell us the way in!"

"Right," said Junie, speaking into the table top from beneath her folded arms. "Corner store?" she said sarcastically. "Gas station?"

"I'm not finished yet," said Marcus with dignity. Junie looked up again, half-heartedly. "You said she was a witch, right?"

"Yes," admitted Junie. "Even she said that. But she's not like a witch in a book, all cackles and warts and stuff."

Marcus was interested. "What kind of witch, then?"

"Well, she can do magic," said Junie, trying to explain. "It's like she's *all* magic, she's a magic person. She doesn't really come from our world, I don't think. She doesn't really belong here."

"Like this garden," said Marcus.

"Yes," said Junie. "That's where she should be, that kind of place. I think she said she was a witch so I would get the general idea, about her magic and everything. But she's — bigger than that. Witch doesn't really say everything there is about her."

"Well," replied Marcus. "She's at least a witch, then. Maybe more. And you said she has this big room full of books, her own private library, right?"

"Yes, so?" said Junie.

"Well, what kind of books do you think they are?"

Junie made the leap at last. "Witch's books," she gasped out, "magic books." She thought of the book about the garden.

"About time, Einstein," said Marcus, matter-of-fact again now. "Come on. We've got to do some research."

Junie, Marcus, and Victoria stood at the door of Miss Quarterberry's house. When Agnes, in her maid's uniform, opened the door at last and looked them all up and down, Junie was prepared. She took a deep breath and said, "Hello. It's me, Juniper Tree."

These words had the desired effect, and Agnes's face relaxed into friendliness in a remarkable transformation. Marcus glanced at Junie, his eyes wide. Junie flushed a little with pleasure.

"These are my friends Marcus and Victoria," Junie continued politely as Agnes smiled and nodded at her. "We were wondering if we could see Miss Quarterberry."

"She ain't here," said Agnes shrugging. " But come in . . . " Junie felt a keen disappointment. "Oh," she said.

"We were hoping we could use her library."

"Oh, goodness, that!" exclaimed Agnes, and Junie didn't know if she was outraged or relieved. "Sure thing, kid, never fear, that's easily done. Off you go, my dears, never fear! You know the way, work or play! Off you go!" And with these strange words of encouragement she disappeared abruptly through a doorway leading out of the hallway. They heard her voice calling heartily, "Off you go! Never fear!"

They looked at one another and laughed. Victoria barked, but Marcus shushed her, and Junie started off whispering, "Off we go!" to Marcus.

"Gosh, I hope I know the way," she said as they followed the turnings of the hallway. "It's a long way away."

"Can't be that far," said Marcus, walking beside her. Victoria's toenails made a click-clicking noise on the polished wood of the floors. "The house isn't that big."

"Oh, it is though," said Junie. "It's sort of like Mary Poppins's carpet bag, I think. Bigger on the inside than the outside." They were still following the hallway, treading all the while on a threadbare Oriental carpet, miles long it seemed, which ran the length of the hallway no matter how often it turned and twisted.

"Nah," said Marcus as he paused to rub up some dust from a window sill with one finger.

"What does that mean?" said Junie crossly.

"It just means," said Marcus, "that this place doesn't seem all that magic to me."

Junie stood glaring after him as he proceeded. Neither of them noticed that the carpet ended abruptly where he walked, and neither of them was prepared for what happened next. Marcus stepped onto the plain wooden floor again as he was speaking, but a panel in the floor slid sideways under his foot and sent him toppling in the opposite direction. "Hey," he said, looking back at Junie as if she was responsible, but she just said, "Look out!"

For the next bit of floor slid sideways the other way, and the entire space seemed suddenly to be made up of moving panels, which heaved and slid and moved under Marcus's feet as if he was in a funhouse.

Victoria yelped, pulling away from Marcus, and skittered to the far side of the crazy floor, where the carpet began again. But Marcus couldn't seem to regain his footing, and he crashed and staggered his way across the moving panels to the safety of the carpet while Junie stood with her hand clapped over her mouth, tears streaming down her face and her shoulders shaking in silent laughter.

"My turn next, I guess," she said, and stepped out gamely onto a panel that heaved like a ship on a swell under her foot. She fell, laughing, onto the next sliding one.

When she reached the other side at last Junie looked at Marcus and shrugged, smiling. They continued along the hallway silently. When Junie glanced behind her she stopped, and nudged Marcus, who stopped and looked around too. The crazy floor was gone, and the dingy carpet stretched unbroken back as far as they could see.

"I think," whispered Junie as if someone was listening, "that she doesn't like to have her magic-ness questioned, if you know what I mean."

"I thought she wasn't even here," Marcus whispered back, glancing around nervously at the innocent walls.

"No," sighed Junie. "She doesn't have to be."

The turnings of the threadbare carpet led them at last to Miss Quarterberry's library. They hesitated together for a moment before the door. Marcus and Victoria looked at Junie expectantly. She took a breath and said, "Well, here we are," and boldly led the way inside.

"Oh," she said, surprised. For it was very dark inside the room today, and the rows of gleaming bookcases she had expected to see made only the quietest of glimmers in the gloom.

"Is there a light switch anywhere?" asked Marcus as he stumbled over one of the piles of books on the floor.

"Maybe," answered Junie, peering around in the darkness. "It's always been light in here before."

"Hang on," said Marcus, and he rummaged in the bulgy bag he had been carrying with him all the while.

"What have you got in there anyway?" Junie asked.

"Supplies," answered Marcus, grinning up at her. "I had a sort of feeling that we might need some stuff." And he pulled his arm back out of the bag, holding a candle and a box of matches.

"Oh, great!" said Junie, impressed by his prudence, and happy too to have him along with her in this dark and suddenly unfamiliar place.

Marcus lit the candle. By the wavering flicker of its light they could see well enough to avoid tripping over the books and papers that cluttered the place, but the strange long shadows that danced along the walls and the ceiling gave the room a new, mysterious aspect all the same.

"It almost feels as if we shouldn't be here," whispered Junie. "As if we're burglars or something."

"Yeah, great, isn't it?" agreed Marcus, holding the candle under his chin so that his face took on the weird reversed shadows of an apparition.

He carried the candle over to a pile of books tipping onto the floor nearby and began to pick them up one by one. He peered at their titles by the scant light, squinting slightly through his glasses.

"Oh, neat," he breathed out in a low voice, and whistled. "Look." Junie in turn peered at the titles: *Spells, Elementary*, she read, and *Charms of Healing; A Magical Grammar; Infusions, Decoctions, and Ointments.* Junie and Marcus looked at each other wondering which book to begin with, when they were startled by a bark from Victoria behind them.

They both wheeled around. There was a rustling in a pile of papers in a corner of the room, and then Junie heard a high-pitched squeaking noise, which excited Victoria even more.

"Mouse in there," gasped Marcus as he tried to grab Victoria away from the tantalizing squeaking. But Victoria barked at him reproachfully and broke free, diving headlong into the pile of papers. Soon her face emerged again, and she looked around the room as if confused. Both the rustling and the squeaking had stopped. "Looks like it got away OK," said Marcus, and Junie was about to agree in relief when they both heard a very small cough behind them and turned around, startled.

A little man stood before them, a little man no taller than Junie, fussing and fidgeting nervously with a pair of spectacles, trying to clean them on the grey, furry sort of cloak he wore. He coughed several times as he did this, a small self-effacing cough directed down at the floor, and his long narrow hands trembled. Junie didn't know whether to be terrified of him or sorry for him.

But Victoria hastened over to where he stood shifting from foot to foot, wagged her tail cheerfully and then stood up on her hind legs and licked his fingers.

The strange little man shrank under this embrace, but patted Victoria's head once or twice, and said, "Well, well, no harm done," in a high, thin voice like a whistle heard from far away. Then he laughed as if he was embarrassed and put his glasses on, where they perched high on the bridge of his long, thin nose, and caught the reflection of the candlelight as it flickered.

13

Mr. Skittery

Junie and Marcus stood looking at the odd little man, and he stood looking at them. None of them seemed to know what to do or say next. But Marcus, perhaps because he found he was a full inch or two taller than the little man, smiled and said, "My name is Marcus, and this is Junie, and this is my dog Victoria."

"Sk-Skittery here," muttered the little man in reply, nodding back at Marcus. "Mi-Mr. Skittery. Sorry about the, ah, the fuss," he went on apologetically, glancing at Victoria. "It's been so long since, since anyone came — came here, where I, that is, such a fuss, such excitement. And hello!" he burst out at last, bowing. Junie and Marcus bowed back, but Victoria simply examined the floor with interest as if they had all discovered something there that she had overlooked.

"You have come for the wart remover, I suppose?" said

Mr. Skittery, and he began to rummage among the papers on the table.

Junie and Marcus looked at one another and shrugged. "I don't think we need any wart remover," said Junie gently to Mr. Skittery, and the little man gazed up at her so sadly that she went on quickly. "But we do need some help, I think," she said, appealing to him. He looked at her suspiciously, as if she might be teasing him.

"We're not really even sure what we're looking for, you know," put in Marcus, "but maybe you could help us."

"Help? Me? You don't know what you're looking for — well, no more do I, you know, no more do I! I never know for absolute certain what I'm looking for, or where it is. So I suppose I might help you, after all, since none of us knows — much of anything!" Mr. Skittery delivered himself of this speech as if following an irresistible line of logic, whose conclusion was inevitable. He was clearly so touched at being asked to help anyone with anything that he could scarcely contain himself, and he trembled in excitement, his bright little eyes twinkling eagerly.

Marcus was gazing around the room at the book-sheves. "Do you have any maps here?" he asked Mr. Skittery. "Maps that tell you, maybe, how to get to, well, to other dimensions?"

Mr. Skittery, after a silent pause, sprang into action as if someone had wound him up and let him go.

"Maps," he repeated with a little leap off the ground which propelled him in the direction of one of the shelves. "Maps. That would be 'M', wouldn't it?" he inquired of Marcus.

"Yes, yes, I guess it would," said Marcus, avoiding Junie's eye and following Mr. Skittery, who stood now peering up at the top of a row of shelves. Junie noticed for the first time that "M" was carved into the wooden panelling at the top of the shelves, almost invisible, wedged right up against the ceiling. I might have known she would arrange even her own library alphabetically, thought Junie, shaking her head wryly.

Mr. Skittery had scuttled off down to a corner of the room, and now he returned, pulling with him a tall ladder with wheels on its bottom. He stopped at the "M" section, panting a little, and proceeded to climb the ladder, stepping gingerly as he ascended. He paused once to glance down at Junie and Marcus on the floor below.

"You will, perhaps, watch if the ladder should crumble?" he whispered, as if his voice alone might cause the rungs to buckle and give way beneath him. "Or if the floor should fail?" he went on, "Or if these shelves should stagger — even if ever so slightly?" The whole ladder trembled as he spoke.

"Yes, of course," said Junie reassuringly. "We'll catch you if you fall, Mr. Skittery. Don't worry."

And Mr. Skittery nodded, frowning, and continued up the ladder. By the time he reached the top he did indeed seem to be very far away above them. He ran his finger along the row of books on the topmost shelf, his other hand meanwhile clutching the side of the ladder.

"Maps, maps, maps," he murmured to himself. Then he began to read out the book titles as he peered at them through his spectacles. Marcus held the candle up as high as he possibly could to help Mr. Skittery see.

The Magenta Magpie, read out the high, whistling voice. *Magic, Elements of; Magnificence, and How to Attain It,* he read, *Animating Mannequins; A Marble in Water, or Magnification; Making Marzipan; Mazes Explained, The Mesopotamian Medusa* . . .

"No maps, I'm afraid," said Mr. Skittery apologetically, looking down at Marcus and Junie. "M-maybe they are out of stock at the moment. Out of stock, or out of order, or out of circulation, or altogether out of reach."

But Junie's curiosity was aroused by the titles Mr. Skittery was reading. "I wonder if we could look at the magic book, anyway," she called up to Mr. Skittery. "It might help," she said to Marcus. "There might be something."

Mr. Skittery was trying now to back down the ladder holding the book Junie had requested. He was reluctant to let go of the ladder with either hand to hold the book, and his cloak kept tangling itself up around his feet and legs as he came down. At last Junie could bear it no longer, and said, "Oh dear, Mr. Skittery, why don't you just toss the book down?"

The little man blinked down at her, took a deep breath, and dropped the book. Junie caught it neatly, sneezing as the dust flew out into her face, while Mr. Skittery reached the floor safely.

But *Elements of Magic* was a disappointment. Junie leafed through its musty, densely printed pages and found it almost unreadable. It might have been one long sentence for all she could tell, looking in vain for chapter headings or even new paragraphs.

As Mr. Skittery led Marcus around the library, pointing out its interesting features as if it were a landscape, Junie peered at the book by the candlelight, unwilling to admit defeat. But soon Marcus appeared beside her and whisked away the candle.

"Hey," she protested, though weakly.

"Food," said Marcus. "All this research stuff has made me incredibly hungry," he went on as he made off with the candle to where his big bulgy bag sat in a corner of the room. He retrieved several brown paper bags which smelt, tantalizing in the dusty room, of sandwiches and fruit and cake.

"You've thought of everything," Junie said admiringly to Marcus as he hauled chairs over to the table and began to empty the bags.

"You think this is for you?" he said, but grinned when Junie's face fell, and said, "C'mon, let's eat."

Victoria had leapt happily up onto the third chair, but Marcus nudged her off, and said, "Mr. Skittery? Would you like any lunch? There's lots."

"Oh, my," said Mr. Skittery softly from where he hovered in the shadows. "Really and truly?"

"Sure," said Marcus. "But you'd better hurry. I'm starved." Mr. Skittery didn't need to be told twice, and he darted to the extra chair quick as a wink.

"Ever so kind," he whistled as Marcus began sniffing waxed paper packages to see what they contained. "Really most generous, you know, I scarcely know what to say, or do, or think." And he blinked in happy bewilderment at Junie and Marcus in turn.

"Cheese," said Marcus, "Peanut butter and jam, peanut butter and banana, tuna, salami, chocolate cake, carrot cake, coffee cake, apple, orange, pear, peach. Help yourself," and he seized a tuna sandwich.

Junie pounced on the salami without regard for manners, but Mr. Skittery's little long fingers very slowly slid out across the table and just as slowly pulled back a cheese sandwich. He did not seize it two-handed and stuff it into his mouth as the children did, but tore small pieces of bread and cheese off the sandwich and ate them furtively, his long nose wrinkling as he chewed in quick little bursts.

Junie was the first to break the silence, unable to contain her curiosity.

"Do you live here with Miss Quarterberry, Mr. Skittery?" she asked.

Mr. Skittery jumped nervously again. "Why, yes, yes, I live here," he answered when he had recovered himself, "though as to 'with', you know, no, I wouldn't say 'with'." And his little head drooped and shook from side to side.

"So you have your own room then?" Marcus asked.

Mr. Skittery seemed more perplexed than offended by this interview, and said, "Yes," looking around at the walls of the library.

"Oh," said Junie, realizing. "You mean right here — you actually live here in the library?"

Mr. Skittery nodded cheerfully at her as if she had just guessed the answer to a riddle.

"Uh, oh," said Marcus then, and the other two followed his gaze down to the floor, littered with crumbs from the feast. "I'll clean 'em up," he offered.

But Mr. Skittery protested graciously. "Oh, no, no, no,"

he said. "No-not to worry, it doesn't matter in the least, not a bit. I-I'll just get them when I'm down — that is to say, don't bother yourself about it, most truly. I'll get them later." And he stood so agitated and earnest before the children, that they sank back down into their chairs without another word about the crumbs.

Marcus gathered up the remains of their lunch and stuffed them back into his bag. Junie looked around at the hundreds of books on the shelves, the floor, and the table, and sighed. They were marvellous, fascinating; she could browse among them for ages, she felt. But they weren't helping her find her way into the magic garden.

"It's no good, Marcus," she said. "We aren't getting anywhere. We'll never find a map here. And we've got to hurry. I've got a feeling I haven't got forever. She hasn't got forever."

"I know," Marcus said reluctantly. "Guess we'd better go back to the drawing board."

But Mr. Skittery was shuffling about a large pile of papers on the table, holding sheets up to the candlelight and peering at them.

"I think we're going to go now, Mr. Skittery," said Junie.

"Maps, marzipan, methuselah," muttered the little man. Then, "Ah!" he said, and held up a large sheet of loose paper. "Not a map, I'm afraid. Just a p-plan, I think." And he held the sheet out to Junie.

Junie looked at it curiously. It was a drawing of something, a little like a maze, a little like a proper map. North, south, east, and west were marked on it in a diagram in one corner, but instead of seas and countries and coastlines, it was made up of straight lines and right angles like the outlines of a maze.

"It's a floor-plan," said Marcus decisively. "A house."

"A house?" said Junie.

"This house," said Marcus, and he pointed to some words near the bottom.

"Mulberry Street," Junie read from the sheet.

And sure enough, following the lines and markings on the plan, Junie saw that it was indeed Miss Quarterberry's house. There was the front path leading up to the door, a long sitting room at the front of the house, and a detailed depiction of the many halls and rooms and staircases and turnings of the place. None of the rooms was labelled, but Junie began to trace her finger up and down the hallways, in and out of rooms, as if she was looking for something.

"Well, it stands to reason," she murmured to herself. "I mean this is where I've seen the garden," she said to Marcus. "Maybe it *is* here somewhere."

"Inside the house?" said Marcus sceptically.

"Nooo," answered Junie, and she spread the plan out on the table and began looking around the walls of the house, half expecting to see small drawings of trees and walkways which might tell her the exact location of the garden. But the plan showed only the house itself, and left little room on the edges of the page for anything else.

Marcus was now leaning over the other side of the table and looking at the plan upside down.

"This must be this room," he said, pointing with a rather grubby forefinger to a small room near one corner of the plan, a room whose walls were drawn in a double thickness.

"See," he said, running his finger along one set of the double lines. "These are the bookshelves, all around the walls.

"Wait," burst out Junie, snatching the plan out from underneath Marcus's finger. For she had seen something. She looked from the plan up to the room around her and back again. She began to turn around, looking at all the walls, then she rushed to each wall in turn and ran up and down, looking, looking.

"Where is it?" she cried out. Mr. Skittery began to tremble more violently than before, but Marcus merely stared back at her, saying, "What on earth are you talking about?"

"The hallway, the hallway," said Junie urgently. "It was here before, here and in the public library, too. Look." And she spread out the plan on the table again and pointed to a place on the lines that Marcus had just traced with his finger. Where Junie was pointing the double lines faded unmistakably, as if they were smudged or partially erased. And directly beyond that weak place in the wall a hallway was drawn in, running behind one of the walls of shelves, and leading — nowhere. The line that stood for the outer wall of the hallway ended abruptly, and was left open-ended, as if whoever made the plan had lost interest, or been called away, or — what?

"Looks like a mistake," remarked Marcus.

"No — it's not a mistake," retorted Junie, full of excitement. "There *is* a hallway here. I've been down it."

"OK," said Marcus. "Where?"

"Well, it used to be right there," said Junie, pointing at

a densely packed bookshelf on the wall directly opposite her. "I know it's there. It's her, you know, it's Miss Quarterberry who does these things. Things are there and then they aren't there. Anyway, it's here, isn't it?" she said, holding up the sheet of paper.

"Calm down, calm down," said Marcus. "I believe you, OK?"

"It leads into her room," Junie mused, touching the place on the floor-plan where the hallway stopped, or began, open-ended. "There's a little room there, like the parlours ladies used to have, in books. And sometimes the hallway starts here, in this room, and sometimes it's in the public library, but it always leads to that room. It's a sort of magic passageway, I think."

"Well," said Marcus. "So maybe somebody forgot to draw in the parlour, or left it out on purpose, to keep it a secret."

"Hmmm," murmured Junie uncertainly. She ran her finger along the hallway yet again, pausing at its open end. She thought of the little parlour, the witch's lair — that small secret room where Miss Quarterberry could be alone.

Secret — or maybe just private — yes, it was private, and she realized all at once how privileged she had been to go into it, to be invited into such a private place. And then, in the first flush of understanding about the little room, she remembered, with a curious little thrill up her spine, another private place. "It was made for privacy," echoed Miss Quarterberry's voice in her mind. And these two things came together in Junie's mind with a sort of click, and she got up all at once, and said, "That's it."

"What's it? What's what?" said Marcus.

"That's it. That's the answer," said Junie decidedly. "Let's go." She began to tidy up the papers on the table in front of her.

"But — " said Marcus as he hastily retrieved his bulgy bag and gently woke Victoria, who had fallen asleep under the table. "You could at least tell me," he complained.

Junie grabbed Marcus's arm and hurried him and Victoria out into the hallway. But when they got there, she said, "Oh, dear, we forgot to thank Mr. Skittery. I'll go back," and opened the door into the library again.

"Mr. Skittery?" she said into the dim room. But no one answered her. He was gone, and she heard only a small rustle of paper on the ground by her feet. She looked down, and saw near the table a small grey mouse eating one of the cake crumbs she and Marcus had dropped there earlier.

Junie bent down a little, slowly, and whispered, "Thank you, Mr. Skittery. Thank you for helping us." The mouse started and looked up at her nervously. It stared at her for a long moment with its bright little eyes, then scurried away in a swift flick, disappearing into the shadows at the far end of the room.

14

Two Conversations

On the way home from Miss Quarterberry's house, Junie tried to explain to Marcus about the hallway.

"Remember?" she said. "Remember I told you about it before. It was the very first thing — it was where all this started, in that hallway."

"But in the library," said Marcus. "The public library."

"Yes, that's where I first found it, but it's a magic hallway, Marcus, obviously."

"Oh, obviously," said Marcus a little resentfully, for he had never even seen it.

"Marcus," said Junie angrily, stopping where she was. "Please don't be like that, believing me and then pretending you don't believe me at all."

Marcus looked down at his feet a little sheepishly. "It's hard to keep it all straight," he complained. "I mean, you say you've done — all right, you have done," he corrected himself when he saw Junie's face, "you've done all these weird things with this weird witch, and you say there's a hallway right in front of me that I can't see, and I don't see what's so important about it anyway. It doesn't have anything to do with me, either," he added, glaring at the ground.

"Oh," said Junie. She realized suddenly how left out Marcus must feel, hearing about her adventures second-hand, not really being involved in them himself. Not like she was, anyway.

"But it does have to do with you, Marcus," she went on, after thinking things over for a minute. "I mean, you're the one who realized the floor-plan *was* a floor-plan, and brought the candle, and the food, and even knew enough to go look in the library in the first place!" She was counting Marcus's contributions off on her fingertips. "And most of all," she said, a little shyly, "most of all it's just been good to be able to talk about it to somebody. I need you, Marcus. Don't go all funny on me."

Marcus regarded her silently for a moment. "It was kind of fun when the floor started moving," he said, starting to smile.

"Yeah," agreed Junie. "Yeah, it was." And she saw that despite all the difficulties, despite her misgivings and uncertainties, she was having more fun than she had ever had. And now Marcus was in it too, which made it even better.

"Tell me again about this hallway, then," said Marcus. "You didn't really tell things all in the right order before, you know. It was all a jumble."

"OK," began Junie. "What I think is this. The hallway's obviously a magic hallway, 'cause it moves around, or at least appears in different places at different times. And it's all full of pictures." She paused. "You know, I bet all those pictures have something to do with the garden," she said earnestly to Marcus as if he had examined every one himself. "I can only really remember two of them, one of the garden — the garden as it was, when those two lived there, and the tree was still standing. That's how the garden should be, except . . . "

"Except what?"

"Well, it's the other picture, the picture of the old man. I told you."

"Yeah, I remember," said Marcus. "Ghoulish, right?" And he made a leering face at Junie. "Creepy crawly. The worms go in, the worms go out."

"No," said Junie, not laughing. "No, he doesn't look dead. He looks — too alive, almost."

"Too alive."

"I can't explain it. He just gives me the creeps, and yet that's who Miss Quarterberry — loves. That's who she wants to be with in the garden." Junie shook her head in confusion.

Marcus shrugged. "No accounting for taste," he said mildly. Junie stared at him in disbelief. But he had never seen the picture after all. He couldn't know.

"Anyway," Junie recalled herself to the subject in hand. "Anyway, all those pictures might have something to do with the garden. But that doesn't matter so much. I think the hallway's the way in to the garden all the same."

"The way in?" asked Marcus. "But you said it led to a little waiting room!"

"Sitting room, not waiting room!" said Junie. "It's not a dentist's office, you know, with plastic chairs and torn-up magazines!"

"Have I been there?" said Marcus, throwing up his hands and unintentionally jerking Victoria away from an interesting beetle on the sidewalk.

"Maybe it is a kind of waiting room, too," Junie mused, ignoring him.

"Well, make up your mind. Magazines, or no magazines?"

"Oh, be quiet for a minute, Marcus. I'm trying to explain it to you."

Marcus made an exaggerated zippering motion across his lips and smiled angelically. Junie groaned.

"The only place I've ever seen, at the other end of the hallway," she went on, controlling herself, "is a little room where Miss Quarterberry goes. It was like a witch's room with a cauldron and everything at first, but then it changed into a sitting room, with chairs and rugs and stuff. No magazines. Do you remember that?"

Marcus, still zippered, nodded hugely.

"OK," said Junie. "But I think it doesn't really matter what it looked like so much as what it was for. It was like — her office, or something."

Marcus raised his eyebrows.

"I just mean, it was like her office because it was her own private room, a place she could go to do magic, or just sit, maybe, if she wanted to. It was private. It was hers. Like the garden."

"Wait a minute," said Marcus, coming unzippered even though Junie shot him a dark look. "Why does that make it the way into the garden? I don't get it."

"I am trying to explain it," said Junie with exaggerated patience. "I don't think it's logical or scientific. This is magic stuff, after all, you know. Why should it be logical or scientific? Here's a magic hallway that leads to a private room. That much we know for sure. I've just realized, I think, just how private that room is. I don't think anybody else ever goes there. Mr. Skittery didn't seem to know anything about it."

"Mr. Skittery didn't seem to know much about anything," said Marcus, smiling a little.

"No," agreed Junie. "He was — he was like a part of the house itself, come alive. That whole house seems to be magic, like one big magic trick of Miss Quarterberry's. So I guess he didn't know much, because if a chair or a picture in one room came alive, what would it know about all the other rooms?"

"Not much," said Marcus.

"But listen," Junie said, "we've got to get this settled about the hallway, Marcus. Miss Quarterberry told me to listen when I felt something in my stomach, like a feeling when you *know* something, though you don't always know why you know. Like — like when you just know Victoria's tangled up in her leash, even though you can't see her."

This seemed to strike an answering chord in Marcus. "I know," he said.

"OK, then. Well, Miss Quarterberry said the garden was made for privacy, and when I saw that floor-plan, with the hallway all open-ended like that, just as if somebody had purposely left something out, to keep it secret and private, then I knew. And you're the one who thought the map might be unfinished to keep the room secret in the first place!" she concluded triumphantly, as if showing Marcus how helpful he had been would convince him once and for all that she was right.

"But what about the waiting room?" said Marcus. "How can it be in the same place this garden's supposed to be?"

"Well, the garden isn't really there any more," reasoned Junie. "At least, not for her. Maybe she made the *sitting room* so the hallway could at least lead somewhere for her. Not just into — emptiness. Nothing."

Marcus was silent.

Junie sighed. "That's all I can think of, anyway. But I know, I just know that somehow that hallway leads into that garden. I can get there that way if I can just go . . . "

"Under the right circumstances." Marcus finished the sentence for her.

"Yes," replied Junie. "The right circumstances." She smiled, and the two walked on silently together.

It was late in the afternoon by the time Junie got home, and the shadows in front of her house were long. Fiona was already home, making up hamburgers in the kitchen to barbecue for supper.

"Where've you been all day?" she asked conversationally as Junie came into the kitchen.

Junie, still deep in thought, had wandered in without

thinking much about what she would tell her mother of the day's activities, and she was caught off guard.

"We went to Miss Quarterberry's," she answered, and then nearly kicked herself when she realized what she'd said.

"Indeed?" teased Fiona. "Get her out to ride bikes with you or play baseball?"

Junie grinned. "She wasn't home."

"Ah," said Fiona, and fortunately became preoccupied in chopping an onion.

"Have fun at Mr. and Mrs. Hedges?" asked Junie, plunking down in a chair and pulling off her shoes, suddenly very tired.

"Yes, thank you," said Fiona. "Things are taking shape, as they say in the topiary business." She waggled an imaginary cigar in her fingers and raised her eyebrows up and down quickly several times.

"Was Mrs. Hedges Alice today?"

"I didn't see her actually. But Harold said she was lying down with a sick headache, so I think she must have been Mary Elizabeth."

"Mum," said Junie then in a tentative voice. "Do you think they're, well, you know, a little weird?"

"Oh, absolutely," answered Fiona promptly. "Nutty as fruitcake."

"But you don't think it matters, that they act so funny?" Junie asked.

"Oh, it matters, of course it matters. It's what makes them what they are. But that doesn't mean it's anything to get upset about. It's just a kind of playing, after all."

"Yeah," said Junie thoughtfully. "That's how I've always thought about it. But I didn't think grown-ups were supposed to play."

Fiona laughed. "Supposed to? There aren't any rules about it, you know. Where is it written, 'At age twenty-one you shall cease to have fun'? Some people just forget how, that's all. I mean, I still play, after all."

"You?" objected Junie, who had never once seen her mother climb a tree or play skipping or turn a somersault.

"Yes, me," answered Fiona in mock defiance. "Look at that table. Why do you think I draw like a maniac?"

Junie looked at the usual tumble of sketchbooks and pencils in front of her. She had never actually wondered why her mother drew pictures, until now.

"Beep," said Fiona. "Time's up. I'm afraid you've missed out on the grand prize of a bus trip up the road and back, the luxurious on-board meal of chips and pop, and the one dollar and twenty-nine cents spending money." She cuffed Junie gently on the top of the head and then spoke in a softer voice. "Because it's fun, silly! Fun! Why do you pretend to be Sherlock Holmes? It's the same thing."

"No, it's not," countered Junie, who didn't see any connection at all between playing Sherlock Holmes and her mother's sketchbooks.

"Not exactly, no, I know," sighed Fiona, sitting down now at the table with Junie. "Look, hon, this isn't a thing we should argue about." She leafed through her sketches idly for a moment. "Mrs. Hedges dresses up in different costumes," she said. "And I draw different costumes. It's not so very different, really. We're both just trying things on, trying things out. And that's playing." She smiled at

Junie. "Oh, that reminds me." She picked up the sketch-books and looked around underneath them, then pulled out a sheet and handed it to Junie. "Here — to put old quarrels behind us."

It was another picture of the boots. Junie looked at it and then back at her mother, inquiringly.

"Yep. You have it," said Fiona. "Look — I've got tons, now, anyway." And Junie watched as Fiona turned over and held up sketch after sketch of the boots, large and small, in half-doodles and finished drawings, over and over again. Junie felt a little frightened at the sight of all these pictures, as if the mysterious boots were taking her mother over, possessing her somehow.

"Why do you keep drawing these?" she blurted out in her burst of worry, forgetting even to say thank you.

"There's gratitude for you," laughed Fiona. "But a fair question, all the same. I don't really know, Junie. I don't usually draw the same thing over and over, do I?"

Junie shook her head mutely, and looked down at the picture in her hands. It was a very good one, she thought absently, and was suddenly touched and very pleased at the gift.

Fiona was looking at another of the pictures. "I think," she began slowly, "that they remind me of Robin Hood. I had a passion for Robin Hood when I was a little girl, you know. Oh, yes," she laughed when she saw Junie's unbelieving face. "I meant to go off and live in the Green-wood, too, and find out all the secret paths through the forest, and right wrongs, and all that."

Watching her mother's dreaming face, Junie suddenly *could* see her mother playing, playing Robin Hood a long time ago, in some wood she had never seen.

"And somehow," Fiona was saying, "when I first sketched out these boots, they made me remember all that, though I didn't mean to draw Robin Hood's boots at all, that I know of. But it took me right back, as soon as I looked at that first sketch and realized what I'd done. And doing them over again brought the feeling back. It's funny — it hasn't faded, I haven't got bored with it or fed up at all. Drawing them makes me feel happy. I am a bit obsessed, I confess. They seem mysterious, to me, almost magical, as if they came from another world." Her eyes were shining.

"They seem like that to me, too," said Junie, looking at the boots. The familiar tingle of fear crept up her spine.

"Do they?" smiled Fiona. "Well, it seems we're both under their spell, then. Do you like the picture?" she asked, shaking herself out of her reverie.

"Oh, yes," answered Junie. "Yes, of course. Thank you." Fiona smiled, and was just getting up from the table when Junie said, "But, Mum," and she sat down again.

Junie had a sudden urge, but she didn't know if she dared act on it. She took a deep breath.

"Could you finish it for me?" she burst out, handing the sketch back to her mother.

"Finish it?" said Fiona, bewildered. "But it is finished, Junie." She looked a little hurt.

"No," said Junie. "No, I know, the boots are finished. They're great. But could you finish the picture? I mean, could you put someone in the boots, somebody wearing them?"

Fiona sighed and ran a hand through her hair. She looked a little pale. "I don't know if I can, Junie," she said. "I never was much good at people, you know."

"But you've been drawing and drawing, and getting better and better. I bet you could draw faces now."

Fiona reached out and stroked Junie's hair. "I didn't know it was so important to you," she said.

"Oh, well, it's just — I love your pictures, Mum, I really do," said Junie. "But they look a bit — empty, or lost, sometimes."

"Unfinished, eh?" said Fiona. "All these years, and you never said a word!" She gnashed her teeth and tore her hair melodramatically, and Junie laughed.

"Well," said Junie then, more seriously. "They're not my pictures."

"No. No, they're not," agreed Fiona solemnly. "But this one is," she said, looking at the sketch she held. "So — I'll give it a shot."

Junie hugged her.

"No promises now," said Fiona, hugging back. "It might turn out terribly, you know."

"No, it won't," replied Junie with certainty. "It will be perfect."

15

A Leak Discovered

By now the dream was almost familiar. Oh, here I am again, one part of her mind thought. But the rest of her was twisted up with excitement in the usual mixture of fear and expectancy. She waited, her eyes scanning the ground and the lower leafy bushes for any signs of the boots. If they should appear already in motion, running towards her, she was ready to flee. But there was nothing. She kept watching the leaves, the ground thick with pine needles, the half-lights and shadows of the night wood. It did not occur to her to wonder where, exactly, she was.

The branches parted and he stood before her. She was surprised; she had been looking in the wrong place. For the first time she saw who wore the boots. And if she hadn't been so terrified, she might have noticed that she wasn't really surprised to discover who it was. She leapt backwards. But he wasn't chasing her this time. He merely stood, stood there in the boots before her, and beckoned. His face was ravaged, horrible — worse even than in the portrait. And he was speaking, his lips were moving, but she couldn't hear him. She saw only the boots before her as always, and the nightmare face, and the lips moving silently, and the arm beckoning, beckoning her in.

She had screamed so loudly this time that Fiona was with her in a moment, cradling and rocking her in her arms as if she were a small child.

"What was it? What scared you?" she was saying as she rocked. "Tell me — it will make it go away."

But Junie couldn't tell her. She leaned up against her mother's warmth and allowed herself to be rocked, but she said nothing.

"Honey?" said Fiona, alarmed as much by Junie's silence as she had been by her screams of a moment before.

"Oh, I can't remember it now," murmured Junie. This was a lie. She regretted the lie, but she knew she had no choice. For if she told her mother about the terrifying man she would have to explain also all her earlier dreams, all that had happened since she met Miss Quarterberry. And it was too late now. She had gone too far alone to turn back now and pull her mother in with her. This calmed her somehow, she didn't know why, this sense that she had a fear that was hers alone, that she couldn't share.

"Feeling better?" said Fiona softly, still slowly rocking.

"Yes, I think so," answered Junie. "It's gone."

Fiona kissed her and tucked her back into bed. "Only

sweet dreams now, OK?" she said, and Junie nodded, smiling slightly.

Lying awake, no longer so frightened, or at any rate frightened only in a distanced, remembering sort of way, Junie thought things over. It had never occurred to her before that the boots might belong to the man in the garden. She was amazed, now, that she hadn't realized it before. Of course it must be him, they must be his boots, she thought. It all seemed crystal clear.

And yet there was a confusion of feelings in her. Drowsily she wondered why this new knowledge — that the green boots belonged to and were worn by the old man in the garden — should reassure her somehow as well as terrify her. It didn't make much sense really. But letting the worry and the confusion drift away from her, she fell asleep again, and slept peacefully until morning.

At breakfast Junie picked up one of Fiona's boot sketches with a sigh of resignation. It was an elementary one, rough, its lines swift and hasty. All right, Junie said to it in her mind. All right, here we are. Now what do we do?

It was just a little harmless sketch, not much more than a scribble, really, or a doodle. Marcus's voice echoed in her mind all at once. "This is a picture of a pair of boots," it was saying. "It isn't real."

"But that's it," she said, dropping the sketch. "They *are* real. I know that now." She smiled up at Fiona who came into the kitchen at that moment.

"No more bad dreams?" asked Fiona over toast and honey.

"No," said Junie. "One was enough."

It isn't real, Junie wrote into her book as carefully as if she were copying a poem. Then she chewed her pencil and looked at the words thoughtfully.

"But they are real," she remarked to the page before her. That was what had calmed her after the terror of her dream the night before. For despite the fear, she at last knew that the boots did belong to someone, were worn by someone. They were no longer just a daydream, something that she had made up. There they were, on the man's feet in the garden. There they were.

"I'd better tell Marcus about this," said Junie, and she went to call him.

"My house," she whispered dramatically into the phone. "I've got it, Watson. Come with speed. All shall be revealed."

"On my way," whispered Marcus back, rising to the occasion. "How will I know you?"

"I'll be wearing a purple coat and smoking a cigar," giggled Junie.

"And I," replied Marcus, "will carry a cane and wear a red carnation."

"Very well," said Junie. "Till then. Take care you are not followed."

"Never fear," said Marcus.

"Oh, not those boots again," groaned Marcus when Junie explained to him about her dream. Fiona had gone to prune somebody's bushes and Junie and Marcus were rummaging in the kitchen for food. Their discussions about the magic garden always made them hungry. Junie was kneeling up on the counter trying to sniff out cookies in the cupboards, and Marcus was plundering the fridge energetically as they talked. He dumped an armload of bread, cheese, grapes, and apples on the table.

Willikins, who had heard the unmistakable noises of food from wherever he had been hiding, proceeded with regal dignity into the kitchen as they talked, and sat in the middle of the floor listening to them.

Junie said, "Hah!" and pounced on a box hidden in the back of the cupboard. She saw Willikins as she clambered down from the counter again.

"Cookie, Willikins?" she said with mock sweetness, holding the box out towards him.

The cat looked away and sighed. Junie ignored him and carried on with the conversation.

"Yes, the boots again," she said. "What is it with you, Marcus?"

"No meat? No cream? No fish or fowl?" said Willikins with dismay, having inspected all the food on the table and settling himself to complain directly in front of Junie's face so Marcus was blocked from view.

"Oh, cat!" said Junie, and she went to the fridge, found a little carton of coffee cream and gave some to Willikins in a dish.

"OK, your majesty?" she said as she set it down.

But Willikins sniffed the cream, turned his nose up, and walked away in silence.

Marcus grinned over the grapes as Junie said, "I give up," and came and sat down again. "Now," she went on. "We've got to work this out, Marcus. I mean, I don't get it. My mum just loves these boots, that's why she keeps drawing them. She thinks they're Robin Hood boots."

"Robin Hood boots?"

"Yes. Like Robin Hood would wear when he was stealing from the rich to give to the poor."

"Do you think they're Robin Hood boots?" said Marcus, evasively.

"No," said Junie. "Well, not exactly. I mean, I never really thought of it until she said it. I think I can see what she means, though."

"You can?"

"Yes. Look, what is it, Marcus? You've got to tell me why you hate them so much."

Marcus gingerly slid a stray sketch of the boots out from under a loaf of bread on the table. He glanced at it for a moment, grimaced and shuddered, and turned it over. Junie looked at him, waiting.

"They just give me the creeps," he said, looking at her helplessly. "I don't know why. But they make me feel as if I'm in a nightmare or something, one of those nightmares where something's chasing you but you can't run away, your legs won't move. They scare me, OK? They just scare me." Marcus looked down a little sheepishly and pushed away the food in front of him. "And whenever I look at a picture of them, my back gets all tingly and I feel as if I ought to run away as fast as I can."

Junie said, "I feel that way, too, Marcus. I've even dreamed what you just said, that they were chasing me and I couldn't get away."

Marcus looked up at her. "But — " he began. "Then, why — "

"But," interrupted Junie, "they also make me feel excited inside like something wonderful is going to happen. Both things," she said, almost to herself. "They make me feel both things."

Marcus was still silent. Junie went on. "And somehow, now, knowing that they're there, in the garden, means I didn't just make them up, and that makes me feel less scared. I don't know why, really. Oh!" She jumped up suddenly, her eyes wide, as if someone had slapped her.

"Marcus," she said. "I think I've got it. Just now, when you were talking — that's just how I feel when I see that picture of the old man, just how I felt in my dream last night!"

"So we're both terrified," said Marcus grimly.

"But not now," said Junie, thumping the table. "Not always. And that picture of the man doesn't always scare people. Miss Quarterberry loves it. And my mum loves the boots!"

Marcus shook his head. "I don't get it."

Junie paced up and down the kitchen rapidly once or twice, thinking.

"Magic leaks," she said at last, her eyes aglow. "Miss Quarterberry said that to me once, she said that magic leaks out sometimes, gets into places it shouldn't be. Maybe it can get into people too, Marcus. Maybe that's what happened here. Listen. We've got some magic boots in a magic garden, and somehow some of the magic leaked out into you, and some into my mum. But you each got only half of it, half of the feelings. See, when I look at the boots, I feel scared like you, Marcus, but I also feel happy like my mum does. I feel both ways. It's like when I look at the picture, I feel just terrified, but Miss

Quarterberry feels just happy."

"But now you say the old man wears these boots," said Marcus. "What's that going to do to all these feelings?"

"Yeah." Junie frowned and sat down again. "I don't know. It makes everything more real, somehow. Sometimes that's good and sometimes it's scary. But at least it's not only scary, not always." She looked up at Marcus hopefully. "Maybe it's been him all the time. Maybe these boots stand for him, the way I'm supposed to stand for the juniper tree. And he is scary," she said. "But maybe not only scary, not all the time. Maybe he's good, too. Maybe he's both."

Marcus took out the picture again and looked at it. "It's funny," he said. "All this fuss about a picture of a pair of boots. It's funny to think about that leaking you were talking about."

"Does it bug you?" asked Junie.

Marcus was still looking at the picture, and Junie realized he wasn't grimacing or looking away. "Not really," he said. "It's kind of neat, really, magic getting inside you. Besides, that means I'm in it too."

"Yes. Thank goodness," said Junie, and they went back to eating once again.

16

Spring Cleaning

> "Oh, boots, oh boots,
> Come off the page,
> Come fit my foots,
> While I'm still the same age."

Junie stood with her hands outstretched over a sketch of the boots, willing them to come alive, to become real boots that she could put on. Nothing. She tried again.

> "Oh boots so kind,
> Oh boots so neat,
> I know you won't mind
> It if you try my feet."

Nothing. Willikins, half-hidden on the window sill behind the curtain, said, "I wouldn't give up my day job, if I were you."

Junie, who hadn't seen him there, chased him out of her room, saying, "Cat, cat! Scat! Scat!" and waving her arms dramatically. When he was gone she sat down on her bed, saying, "Well, that one worked, anyway."

She sighed; it wasn't working. I don't know the right spell, she thought, and I'm not a witch anyway. I need Miss Quarterberry to help me. But she can't help me, she said that. "Aargh," she groaned, and fell back onto the bed.

She knew, she thought now, all she needed to know. If she could somehow get the boots out of the picture and put them on, and wear them down the magic hallway, she would be able to get into the garden. At least, she thought so. She was a little uncertain about how the boots could be worn by the man in the garden and by herself at the same time, but she pushed this worry out of her mind. She wanted to wear those boots into the garden. "I've even more or less been invited," she said, thinking of her dream about the man beckoning her. She was still frightened of him, but somehow her talk with Marcus about the boots had calmed her down.

He *was* dangerous, probably, and Junie didn't know what she would do if and when she had to meet him face to face. But she had by now become almost accustomed to her fear, and felt it was somehow manageable. It was still there, living down in her belly and rumbling like hunger from time to time, but it was a small, hard thing like a swallowed marble, not a looming, nameless dread as it had been before.

Besides which, she was concentrating on practical things now, like doing research and trying to conjure pencilled boots off paper. Despite the fact that she was having no success at all with the boots, she felt generally grown up and competent. She felt she ought to be wearing glasses and writing important things on clipboards.

The summer was waning. It was still hot, and everything looked much the same, but there was a certain indefinable settling and sagging of the season, as always happened in August. School would begin again soon, and Junie was anxious to finish her task before then. Sometimes a small sadness came to her these days, in idle moments. She tried to shake it off, or told herself she simply missed seeing Miss Quarterberry. What she knew, but would not let herself truly realize, was that if she did it, if she managed to get into the garden, she would very likely never see Miss Quarterberry again. But she wasn't ready to believe this, not yet, and so she kept herself absorbed in clipboard thoughts and refused the small sadness entry when it came knocking at her mind.

She looked again at the sketch. It looked like just a bunch of pencil lines on paper. She had been looking at it for too long, thinking about it too hard. Now, like a phrase repeated over and over again, it had become flat and meaningless, telling her nothing.

Fiona looked into Junie's room and saw her lying on her bed.

"Bored?" she said.

"No. Yes. I don't know," said Junie.

"I'm going over to the Hedges' house soon," said Fiona. "Want to come too?"

"Yes," said Junie, sitting up. "Yes, that'll be fun." I'm

not getting anywhere, she thought. Might as well go out for a while.

The Hedges didn't disappoint her. As they approached the house, Junie saw that some of the topiary shapes on the hedges surrounding the Circus were nearly complete. And again she had a sense of time passing, pressing her to finish her own job, too.

When Mrs. Hedges came to the door, Junie watched her anxiously to see who she was. She was hoping for jolly Alice once again. But the grey-haired woman who threw open the door as if she had been waiting just behind it appeared to be Mary Elizabeth.

Mary Elizabeth was the organizing force of the small crowd known as Mrs. Hedges, and when she was not ill, she was formidable. Today she stood before Junie and Fiona resplendent in bright orange gardening gloves and an immense straw hat held firmly on her head with a purple scarf tied under her chin.

"I swear," she boomed out at her guests as if continuing a conversation already in progress, "these sick headaches are a restorative force to me. A restorative force!" she shouted again as if Junie and Fiona might not have heard her the first time. "They creep up slowly, you know, Mrs. Summers," (Mary Elizabeth always called Fiona 'Mrs. Summers'), "and pounce upon me from behind and lay me low for a day or so, but afterwards I'm up again better than ever."

Junie half expected her to pound her chest in a display of her new-found strength like some great ape. But Mary Elizabeth merely strode through the house with a stately, forceful gait, and led Junie and her mother towards the Circus. "We are spring cleaning the Circus," she said decisively.

"Spring cleaning?" asked Fiona. "In mid-August?"

"Never got to it in May," answered Mrs. Hedges. "But better late than never, I always say. Harold, I'll venture, has lost no time in deserting his digging," she confided, lowering her voice so that she spoke at a normal human volume. "But we'll pounce on him, shall we, and set him straight. I'll show him," she said, rubbing her orange gloves together in anticipation. "If he's bouncing, I'll cook tonight!" And she flung open the kitchen door triumphantly, saying, "Aha!"

Mr. Hedges was indeed bouncing, and Junie didn't know whether to clap in delight as she saw him going up and down on the trampoline, or feel sorry for him now that he was to be punished with Mary Elizabeth's cooking. He looked like a rubber ball in the shape of a man. He was wearing a strange outfit, a sleeveless affair which covered his body and legs to the knees, brilliantly striped top to bottom in yellow and blue. It looked like a very old-fashioned kind of bathing suit.

When he saw Junie and Fiona appear he waved, spoiling a somersault he was about to make, and shouted,

"Hell — " up,

"o," down.

"Wel — " up,

"come," down.

"My dears," up. This was shouted out very quickly before he descended. Junie clapped, and Mr. Hedges sprang gracefully off the trampoline, grabbed a towel, and sauntered over to issue a more formal welcome.

Mary Elizabeth stood, hands on hips, glaring at him.

"My love," said Mr. Hedges, not in the least disturbed. "An interval of recreation. Welcome," he said to Junie, and shook her hand cordially.

"Liver tonight, Harold," said Mary Elizabeth. "Mark my words." And she stalked off towards Fiona, her immense hat sailing through the air like a great ship on top of her head.

Mr. Hedges sighed. "Ah, well," he said. "This is the price of lightheartedness, I suppose. Leathery liver instead of *Boeuf Bourguignon.*" He winked at Junie and hopped with amazing speed into a large overall which covered his bathing suit, zipped it up, seized a shovel which was close by, and reported for duty to his wife, saluting smartly and clicking his heels together.

Spring cleaning, it appeared, consisted mainly of a major rearrangement of all the flower beds, and a general weeding, trimming, polishing and beating of the entire Circus into submission. Just at the moment a great many flowers and bushes sat forlorn and uncertain on the grass, having been uprooted with great clumps of earth still clinging to them, and quite a few astonished worms, waiting to be carried off and replanted in their new beds.

Fiona took a spade and cheerfully began to help, while Mary Elizabeth waved her arms about directing the operation like an orchestra conductor. Junie looked about for a spade, too, but there weren't any more, so she helped instead by carrying the displaced plants and flowers to wherever Mrs. Hedges instructed. She stroked their leaves gently as if to comfort them in the trauma of their change of residence, and was careful to retrieve all the stray worms that went with them, so as not to break up any families.

"What on earth?" shouted Mary Elizabeth at one point, as if she had just been told Mrs. Battle was about to invade the Circus. She stood by a small corner flower bed and gazed accusingly down at a small evergreen bush that huddled in one corner as if cowering away from her.

"What is it, my love?" asked Mr. Hedges as he hurried over to her. Fiona and Junie came along too.

"How did that get in here?" she demanded, pointing at the bush as if it might have crept in from off the streets like a stray dog, to take up illicit residence in her flower bed.

Harold scratched his head. "I believe we planted it, my love, a year or two ago," he said.

"Never!" boomed Mary Elizabeth. "Truly?" she said then.

Harold nodded and shrugged. "Hmph," said Mary Elizabeth, relenting a little, but she soon mustered all her forces once again after this temporary lapse into uncertainty, and said, "Well, it will never do. This bed has already been reserved for the Bleeding Hearts."

Junie felt sorry for the little bush, and asked Fiona, "What is it?"

"Juniper," said Fiona, as if she too was feeling sorry.

"Juniper?" said Junie. "That's a juniper?"

"Yes," said Fiona, surprised at Junie's excitement. "Not a very healthy one, though, I'm afraid."

"No," agreed Mary Elizabeth as Harold dug in his spade and began to uproot the little bush. "It hasn't taken at all well. We shall have to get rid of it. It won't do."

"Get rid of it?" asked Junie, braving Mary Elizabeth's bluster in her anxiety. "You mean throw it out? Let it die?"

"Compost heap," assented Mary Elizabeth.

"Oh, could I have it?" pleaded Junie with a sudden urgency. "Could I have it to grow for myself, since you don't want it anyway? It's just . . . I'd hate to see it die."

"Sentiment," said Mrs. Hedges, "has no place in spring cleaning. Mark my words!" But then she turned her back on the bush, and said, "Oh, very well. I'll fetch a pot."

And in the end it was Mrs. Hedges herself who planted the bush in a pot and watered it and presented it to Junie with great ceremony, and with a great many instructions for its care and feeding.

Junie carried the juniper home when she and Fiona left later in the afternoon, and placed it in a sunny corner of her own room. It was indeed a bedraggled-looking little bush, with several brownish branches, but Junie propped it up encouragingly and told it to keep its chin up, though where the chin might be on one small, newly-rescued juniper bush, she couldn't say.

When she went downstairs to set the table for dinner, she found that Fiona had already set it. She had more than set it, in fact, for there was a tablecloth on the table tonight, a candle burning, and a rectangular package wrapped up and tied with ribbon, sitting on her plate. Fiona had even, in a burst of festive feeling, tied some ribbon around Willikins' neck, and he sat on one of the chairs looking like a gift himself, and blinking in gracious acknowledgement of any well-deserved compliments that might come his way.

"What's all this?" said Junie, pausing in surprise at the kitchen door.

"All Hail the Rescuer of Juniper Bushes!" Flona cried, tooting out a fanfare on an imaginary trumpet.

"It's not even my birthday," said Junie, smiling.

"No, but it doesn't matter. A little celebration of nothing now and then is good for the soul," replied Fiona.

"And what's this?" asked Junie, picking up the present that lay on her plate.

"For you. Open it."

And Junie slowly undid the ribbon and pulled away the crinkly paper, realizing as soon as she saw the edge of the frame what the present was going to be. "Oh, you've finished it!" she exclaimed, looking up at her mother before she pulled off the last of the paper to look at the picture itself.

"Yes," Fiona sighed and smiled a little hesitantly. "Now don't get your hopes all up, Junie," she said. "It's been years since I've drawn people, you know, and I don't know if this is what you had in mind or not." She seemed nervous all of a sudden, and Junie stopped smiling, too, as she freed the picture from the paper and leaned forward to look at it by the flickering light of the candle.

"Oh," she said, for the first thing she noticed was the colour. The whole picture was drawn with coloured pencils, and this in itself was so unusual in one of Fiona's pictures that she looked up at her mother in surprise.

"The colour," she said.

"I know," exclaimed Fiona with a smile, as if she had surprised even herself with what she had done. "I thought, well, since I'm plunging into people, I might as well go the whole way and try some colour too. And you know, Junie, it was such fun! I think I'll go on with it now, keep drawing people. This picture — well, drawing this picture was like crossing a kind of barrier for me, and I don't think I ever want to go back again."

Junie gazed at her mother's rapt face, and said, "And all because of those boots."

"Yes," agreed Fiona. "Those wonderful boots."

It was a young man who stood now in the magic boots, a young man dressed in woodland greens and browns, with a quiver of arrows slung over one shoulder and a bow in his hand.

"Robin Hood," said Fiona. "Close as I could get, anyhow."

But is it? thought Junie. She had been looking at the boots, wondering at how closely they matched the luminous green colour they always were in her dreams. And amazed at how easily and naturally they fitted the young man, how well they looked, as if they should have been there all along. Suddenly all the other pictures and sketches of the boots seemed only partial, unfinished things, foolish things. She couldn't remember, now, how she could ever have been frightened by them.

But when her mother said "Robin Hood", Junie bent to look more closely at the young man's face. Was it Robin Hood? It looked oddly familiar to her, and she frowned, puzzling over the curly brown hair and beard, the half-smile on his mouth, the joyful green eyes.

"Well, Robin Hood to me, anyway," said Fiona, breaking Junie's silence. "He might be someone else to you."

Someone else to you. Could it be? Junie narrowed her eyes at the picture, trying to imagine how that face might look if it were older, lined and haggard, scarred by despair and so drained of colour that even the eyes might seem to be no colour at all. She squinted at the picture until the eyes seemed to be gazing back at her and in that moment she knew.

Fiona, dishing up chicken and potatoes and beans, made a face at Junie, and said, "Well, you might at least tell me if you like it or not!"

Junie couldn't believe it. How could her mother have drawn the man in the garden without ever seeing him? And not merely drawn him, but drawn him young and happy again, all the pain gone from his face, green-eyed and more than human, finally — whole.

"I think it's the most beautiful thing I've ever seen in my whole life," she said quietly.

"Good heavens," said Fiona, blushing. And then she plonked Junie's dinner down in front of her and said, "Well, that's all right then."

17

Ready

It was a kind of completion, like the healing of an old, deep ache. The first thing Junie saw when she opened her eyes the next morning was the picture of the young man in the green boots, smiling at her. She sat up hastily and looked at it.

"I don't have to wear the boots," she said aloud, speaking to the picture. "You already do. They're yours. They're where they should be." The picture, being just a picture, sat there and said nothing in reply, but Junie felt she had finally understood something.

The day was golden, sunny and silent. Even the birds in the trees outside seemed to speak in quieter voices than usual, so as not to disturb the prevailing hush. Junie wandered through the house restlessly, a feeling of anticipation and uncertainty making her unable to settle. She watered the little potted juniper and carried it outside into the sunshine, went back inside and got the picture and the half-coin symbol and set them beside the juniper on the grass. Then she sat down and looked at them. The glass in the picture frame gleamed at her. The small symbol glowed and looked pearly and precious in the sunlight. And the little juniper, already looking healthier and greener, seemed to shine, too.

I'm putting things back together, thought Junie. Like a puzzle. I'm getting all the pieces and putting them back together so they're one whole thing again. Marcus has been helping, and my mum has been helping, too, without knowing it. But I've got all the pieces now, and I think I'm ready. And I think that all this time while I've been trying to work out how to get into the garden, I've really just had to realize that the garden is in me. It's right here inside me.

She thought of the first juniper tree, the one whose namesake she was. She remembered how Miss Quarterberry had told her that that first tree took care of the garden, and watched over it, and somehow held it inside itself, held it all together. And since I'm that juniper tree, too, thought Junie, then I have the garden inside me just the way it did. I have it inside me because I'm the only one who can see it, who knows how it's supposed to be, who knows how to put the pieces together. And it's knowing that that's important. That's what I had to find out all along.

So many lost things, broken things, she thought mournfully. The tree that fell, and died because it was real. The little half-coin symbol, broken in two, waiting to be joined again to its other half. Just like Miss Quarterberry, thought Junie. She can't even see her garden, now, and that's like being broken, too. And all those pictures in the magic book about the garden, even those were incomplete, faceless, or voiceless, missing something.

Even the boots. All those pairs of boots, in pictures and in dreams, that were part of a bigger picture all the time. But I didn't know that, thought Junie. Maybe I didn't want to know that. I think I wanted the boots to be mine, but I was afraid of them because they were his. He made the storm, after all, that killed the juniper tree. No wonder I was so afraid of him! She closed her eyes, and remembered the tree falling in the magic book, remembered that it had pained and horrified her as if she herself were falling, as if her own roots were torn, her own branches broken, her own trunk severed and destroyed, never to stand again.

Maybe I wanted the boots to run away in, she mused wryly, forcing herself to open her eyes again. But trees don't get to run away. They have to stay where they are, in one place. It wasn't that, anyway. I wanted them because they were his, too, because they're in the garden and they're his. And I know — she took a deep breath — I know that no matter how often Miss Quarterberry calls me Juniper Tree, I still won't ever be a real tree living in that garden. I won't be able to stay there with them.

But you will, she said to the little juniper in front of her. You're one piece. And you're another, she said to the symbol. And you! She picked up the picture. You're already there, hidden inside all the pictures, good and bad, and I just had to see you like this, to see how you were meant to be, to put all the other pieces together. The picture, I get to keep. That's something. And if my mum thinks you're Robin Hood, it doesn't matter, does it, because you and I know better.

And then Junie was crying, crying with her head bent down on her knees. She was crying for the garden, for Miss Quarterberry, for the dead juniper tree, for all the half-pictures and broken things, and for herself, most of all perhaps. Crying because it was nearly over, she knew, and there was nothing more she could do but finish it, help it to be over, though that was the last thing she wanted in all the world.

In the late afternoon Junie got ready to go. She pocketed the half-coin symbol, put the picture back in her room, called Marcus on the phone, left a note for her mother, and picked up the little juniper to carry with her to the library. Just as she was about to shut the door behind her, she saw Willikins sitting on the couch in the living room and she paused, looking at him.

"Goodbye, Willikins," she said solemnly.

"Going to seek your fortune?" replied Willikins. "About time, I should say, well out of your kittenhood as you are. I've been waiting for that room of yours to be vacated for years now, but no, you just keep staying and staying — "

Junie smiled and closed the door on his voice.

In the park she met up with Marcus. "The new juniper," she said when he looked questioningly at the pot she carried in one arm. Then she explained as well as she could about what she had discovered, and what she had realized, and found out she knew all along. "I'm sorry you can't come too, Marcus," she finished.

"Me, too," he shrugged. "But I'll walk with you to the library anyway."

And they crossed the park together in silence. At the big glass doors, Junie said, "You might as well come in, too. Might get to meet Miss Quarterberry at last!" So, since Victoria had remained behind, Marcus went in too.

"Oh, no," said Junie as soon as they got inside. She had expected, maybe even hoped, that the library would be quiet and solemn and church-like inside, to match her mood. But she and Marcus were met by a wall of sound inside, a great roar like a wave engulfing them. It was the old crowd once again, ranged in a formal semi-circle by the picture books and singing. "Shine on, shine on harvest moon," they sang in perfect, deafening harmony. Junie and Marcus looked at one another.

"Looks like some choir or something meets here," remarked Marcus bewildered.

"No, no," said Junie, exasperated. "They're hers." But she too was confused. She had been so sure Miss Quarterberry would be waiting here for her, preferably dressed like a nun, wilting by a lighted candle or two, that she was completely overwhelmed by the noise and the crazily familiar crowd of bespectacled faces. Usually, too, the sight of them meant Miss Quarterberry was not available, not to be reached by Junie or anyone else, so that now Junie didn't know whether to feel frightened or elated. For the music was, after all, the music, and in spite of herself she felt a bubble of joy rising up in her in response to the wave of singing voices.

As they stood watching the singers, Junie recognized

Agnes among them, and in the same moment saw her detach herself from the front row and approach them, still singing. She tried to smile around her voice, which poured out of her mouth at a surprising volume, and beckoned and gestured Junie and Marcus to come and sit down on two of the small children's chairs that were scattered by the picture books.

So Junie and Marcus sat down like a tiny audience at an immense recital, and listened to the singing. There didn't seem to be anything else to do.

They watched the singers, and after a little while Junie began to wonder where the conductor was. They looked a little unfinished without a conductor, like a glove without a hand in it. And then she looked more closely at their faces and saw that they were all looking at the same spot, somewhere behind and above Junie's head. All their glasses seemed to gleam in unison, in one direction. Junie turned around.

She was there, standing, amazingly, on the topmost shelf of a book stack, and conducting her singers imperturbably. Junie nudged Marcus, thinking at the same time it was a good thing the ceiling was high. Miss Quarterberry wouldn't look nearly so grand if she had to crouch up against the ceiling like a frog, with her knees around her ears. Marcus looked at Junie after seeing the apparition up in the air, and Junie nodded. They both grinned. Miss Quarterberry, looking as cool and reserved as on the first day Junie had met her, waved her arms in measured beats as the singing went on, and nodded unsmilingly at Junie and Marcus, acknowledging their presence.

The singing went on. Junie and Marcus clapped, a little self-consciously at first, after each song was finished. But their clapping brightened all the singers up so obviously, making them grin and nudge each other bashfully, that soon Junie and Marcus were clapping louder and longer, and trying to whistle in appreciation.

After a while Junie noticed that it was getting dark. She didn't know how long they had been there, whether it was a few minutes or hours and hours. It didn't seem to matter any more. She had glanced back at Miss Quarterberry once or twice, wondering vaguely how she was going to get down from the top of the book stack. But otherwise she was concerned about nothing, not bored or frightened or worried or even confused any more. When she looked at Marcus he seemed to be a long way away, but then he turned and smiled at her and she smiled back and was happy he was with her.

The singers were swaying now, Junie noticed, rocking back and forth together slowly, until some of them got out of time with the rest and began to bump into each other. They would giggle and start swaying again, but soon they were all so hopelessly out of step with each other that they seemed like splashing water, bouncing off in different directions. They moved apart, still singing, to avoid knocking one another unconscious with their jolting and bumping, and before Junie knew it they all seemed to be dancing, joining hands and forming a circle.

Somebody took her left hand, and Marcus took her right hand, and they were dancing, too, part of the circle. Most of the singers had stopped singing, now, to save their breath for dancing, but still there was music, loud music in the air all around them. And everyone kept bumping his neighbour, and stepping on toes, and saying, "Oomph," or, "Excuse me," or, "I'm terribly sorry," and laughing at their own clumsiness, and dancing the whole time, all gallantly trying to keep time to the music, which became wilder and more complicated every moment.

Despite the shadowy light, Junie looked around, laughing, and thought, It doesn't seem very mysterious or magical at all, but this must be some kind of spell we're all in. Everyone around her reminded her, more than anything else, of a bunch of grown-ups entangled among their shopping-carts at the supermarket, all trying to manoeuvre politely but ridiculously around each other. But here they all were, holding hands and dancing in a dim and empty library while Miss Quarterberry conducted from on top of a bookshelf.

But the bookshelf was empty now. Soon enough she caught sight of Miss Quarterberry on the opposite side of the circle, kicking up her heels as high as anyone, and holding hands with Agnes on one side and one of the dignified middle-aged gentlemen on the other. She caught Junie's eye and held it, looking at her very intently and smiling a little. Then she broke away from her partners all at once and came and drew Junie out of the dance as well.

The others closed ranks and continued dancing, but Miss Quarterberry led Junie away to a quiet corner and they both stopped and looked at one another, panting a little from their exertions. Then Miss Quarterberry bent and put her arms around Junie and hugged her very close for a moment. In that instant Junie again thought, as she had once before, that Miss Quarterberry was somehow transformed, become young and lovely and shining. And as they moved away from one another, Junie swore she saw a pair of white arms brush against her own, and a pair of white hands glittering with rings. But Miss Quarterberry, before her again, was wearing an unmistakably long-sleeved dress, and no rings at all.

"Juniper Tree," she said very softly. "You are ready?"

Junie nodded, but found she could say nothing. She searched Miss Quarterberry's face, trying to memorize its features. But Miss Quarterberry read her anxious expression and said, "Don't be morbid, child," in quite her old manner.

And then she simply took Junie's hand and walked with her back towards the others. Without looking at Junie, and speaking as if she was making a remark about the weather, she said, "You have done more for me than you will ever know." Junie felt a pressure on her hand, and then it was released.

They found the others had stopped dancing and were now congregated around a long table covered with great platters of fruit. Junie couldn't remember seeing the table before. Everyone was holding a large goblet like the one Junie had once drunk a magic potion from, and eating. Every imaginable kind of fruit was spread on the table — strawberries, raspberries, blueberries, peaches, plums, oranges and apricots — all piled high on the platters and gleaming like edible riches.

Someone thrust a goblet into Junie's hand as well and she drank thirstily. "What is it?" she asked as Agnes refilled her goblet from a large pitcher, but Agnes merely winked and said, "Ah, now that would be telling," and faded back into the milling crowd.

Junie looked around. Somebody had placed large candles on the table now, and their flames, and the moving shadows, at last made the place feel magical, and mysterious. Catching sight of Marcus, Junie went to join him, and found that he was sitting on the floor, eating peaches, and chatting happily with Mr. Skittery.

Mr. Skittery jumped up and bowed several times at Junie's approach, but Marcus just said, "This is great! You didn't tell me there was going to be a party."

"I didn't know," said Junie.

"No more did I, you know," put in Mr. Skittery eagerly, his little bright eyes sparkling. And he nibbled a strawberry as if he had said all he could possibly be expected to say, and could now relax and enjoy himself.

"Did you see any plums up there?" asked Marcus, craning around Junie to get a glimpse of the table.

"I think so," answered Junie absently, but Marcus looked down and found a bowl of plums sitting in front of him. "Oh, my gosh," he said, gazing at them, and then reached out to take one as if he thought they might disappear.

Junie didn't feel like eating, though she found the smell of the fruit all around her very sweet and heady, and she walked away after a while, leaving Marcus saying the names of various kinds of fruit and hearing his, "Oh, my gosh," as bowl after bowl appeared in front of him.

She left the crowd and went to fetch the little juniper

from where she had left it by the door. As she turned back with it in her arms she saw everyone standing facing her, smiling, goblets raised. They had stopped talking, and Miss Quarterberry, standing in front, held up her goblet highest of all and said, "Juniper Tree."

"Juniper Tree," repeated everyone else, toasting her, and they smiled and drank.

But Junie frowned. She didn't want all this attention, all this kindness. "But I haven't done anything yet," she protested, louder than she meant to, and to her surprise everyone burst out laughing. "She says she hasn't done anything yet," they repeated to one another, and laughed the more. Junie shook her head and turned away, thinking things weren't going at all the way she had expected them to go. But Miss Quarterberry was waiting for her at the entrance to one of the corridors leading away from the crowd, and she beckoned Junie towards her.

"Pretend it is all a dream, if it will help you, child," she said. Marcus appeared beside her, and took Junie's hand a little awkwardly. His mouth was stained with plum juice. "Make sure you remember everything, so you can tell me after," he whispered, and then he patted her shoulder encouragingly.

"And now, with my best love, farewell," said Miss Quarterberry. And Junie was alone, alone with the books all around her as she had been the very first day she had come to the library and met Miss Quarterberry.

Surely that couldn't be it. "Wait a minute," she said, a thousand questions crowding into her mind. She ran back into the open space. But it was empty. The table, the fruit, the people were gone, the music was stilled, even

Marcus was gone. Suddenly Junie was frightened, and she called, "Marcus? Marcus?" looking around wildly and clutching the little juniper tightly to her side.

There was no answer, but in the newly dark room she saw a flicker of light, and there was Mr. Skittery coming towards her with a candle in his hand, nodding and bowing as he approached.

"Where is everyone? Where's Marcus?" Junie demanded.

Mr. Skittery shrank back a little, but said, "Oh please, please don't fret, miss, don't fret yourself. I've been sent to show you the way, you know, and all the rest don't matter. M-Mister Marcus, I should think, has been taken home or some such place. She wouldn't lose him, you know, oh dear no, dear, dear, dear."

Mr. Skittery seemed so flustered and concerned, that Junie found herself becoming calm again, watching his face all screwed up with anxiety. She let him go on a little longer, and finally smiled at him and followed him as he led the way through the corridors and book stacks of the empty library to the hall of pictures.

At the entrance to the hallway he stopped and nodded at her. "Here it is, here we are," he said. And then, since Junie said nothing in reply, he looked at her as kindly as he could, and through a great effort of will, offered some words of encouragement. "I-I wouldn't worry if I was you," he said. And then, thinking better of this, he said, "Well — actually — well, I probably would worry if *I* was you. But as I'm not you, and you're not me, but are instead, you know, *you*, well then — why worry?" And he nodded triumphantly at

her as if he must certainly have dissolved any little
anxiety she might be feeling, and waited kindly as she set
off alone down the hall.

18

Into the Garden

Once, twice, three times during that long, solitary walk down the magical hall of pictures, Junie paused, and turned, and saw Mr. Skittery still standing at the entranceway. Each time he bobbed and nodded as he saw Junie turn to look at him, and she found the courage she needed to keep going.

She arrived at the tall, carved door at last, and reached out to open it, not allowing herself to hesitate. But to her surprise it was locked. She stepped back and stared at it, amazed. "Well, how on earth — " she cried out into the hallway. She stopped, hearing the echo of her own voice — "on earth, on earth, on earth" — as it bounced back at her from the walls around her. She peered back down the dim hallway, but Mr. Skittery was gone.

Looking at the door once again, she noticed for the first time a keyhole just below its shining knob. She put down the little juniper and bent to look through it, feeling rather silly. She could see nothing — the keyhole was only a small dark slot anyway. Stuffing her hands in her pockets, she felt the smooth and jagged edges of the half-coin symbol against her fingers and she brought it out of her pocket and looked at it.

"Hmmm," she said, eyeing its blue-green surface and the keyhole once again. And then, without thinking, she tried sliding the symbol into the keyhole. It fit, its jagged side obviously meeting up with some mechanism inside the door, and Junie heard an encouraging click. She pulled the symbol out again and turned the doorknob. It moved, this time, and the door opened an inch or two. Hastily, her heart racing, Junie stuffed the symbol back into her pocket, picked up the juniper, and pushed through the doorway.

Junie had heard the door slam shut behind her, slam shut in a great rush of wind that hit her full in the face as soon as she stepped through. But she couldn't see the doorway any more, or anything else, for she was standing in darkness. She stood absolutely still as if she had been struck blind, and clutched the little juniper to her side to keep it from being blown away in the wind, and tried to think where she might be.

Everything was wrong. Junie had expected to step through the doorway into sunlight and the scent of flowers, to see the enchanted lawns of the magic garden stretching away before her, and to be greeted, very likely, by a swoon of violins announcing her triumphant entry. But she stood here in utter blackness with a mournful wind like a restless ghost buffeting her on all sides, and panic rising in the back of her throat. Her only thought was that something had gone terribly, horribly wrong with the magic, and that the doorway had led her into the wrong place.

And her terror reached up and clutched her by the throat and she panicked outright. Surely, she thought in that moment, Miss Quarterberry was an evil witch who had lured her here to destroy her. Mr. Skittery and all the others were evil spirits who had deceived her with false kindness, and hypnotized her with their music and their dancing. Probably there never was a garden at all. No, she was sure of it now. There never was such a place at all, and she had been duped and fooled and led on into this trap, and she would never, ever get out of it again.

She wheeled around, and began to run, choked with fear, looking for the way back, the door into the hallway. But in the darkness she had lost her bearings, and she ran here and there blindly, confusing herself even more, sure she would never find her way home again.

She stumbled, soon enough, running blind as she was, and fell sobbing, utterly lost, onto the ground. The little juniper fell with her, and as she stretched out her arms, clutching the earth as if she was clinging to the edge of a cliff, she found it with one hand, lying on its side and half sliding out of its pot. But she didn't care. She had been a fool over it anyway, a ridiculous fool to carry around a potted bush like a security blanket, as if it meant something, as if it could help her, as if it were anything more than a bunch of twigs in dirt.

Junie lay there, crying and railing against herself for

being such a fool, until her tears, as tears will, began to run out. She became quieter then, but still didn't move, until after a while she began to feel a little silly, lying there on the ground. No one was hurting her, after all. She seemed to be completely alone.

She sat up and wiped the tears off her face. Then she set the little juniper upright again and scooped as much of the soil as she could back into its pot and looked around. And only then did she realize that she could, now, look around. Either it wasn't as dark as it had been, or her eyes had grown accustomed to the light, but she could make out something of the place she was in.

She was outside somewhere, but she knew that already from the feeling of openness around her, the rushing of the wind through the air, and the smell of earth and dampness. The sky, she could see now, was rimmed with a pale greyish light and pricked with stars. The stars looked very far away, to her, and she didn't know enough about constellations to be able to tell if they looked like the stars on earth, or the stars of some other world.

A large open, rolling space stretched out all around her, featureless and eerie. It seemed like a kind of desert, except that Junie was sitting on grass, a short, springy turf. Several large tufts of it lay on the ground where she had torn them up while she was crying. Looking around quickly, Junie scanned the air around her for the door she had come through, half expecting to see it standing on the grass like some weird sculpture, a door without walls. But there was nothing.

It was a desolate place, the wind still rushing by, from nowhere into nowhere, and in the middle of it Junie felt desolate, too. Her fear was gone, but it had left behind only a sense of dry emptiness like the waste place all around her. And when the thought came into her mind, again, that she was stranded and lost and might never find her way home, it was a neutral thought like a fact, now, a piece of information arousing neither joy nor sorrow.

Still the wind was blowing, flowing over the emptiness of the place like a river of air. Junie's legs began to tingle, and she moved them and stood up slowly, as if she were bruised and battered all over. Vaguely, she began to wonder what she ought to do now, now that she had tried, but failed, to reach the magic garden for Miss Quarterberry. Magic gardens, Miss Quarterberry — it all seemed to have happened a long time ago now. And she shrugged as she realized she could not even call to mind the image of Miss Quarterberry's face.

She picked up the juniper and began to walk, squinting ahead in the darkness to keep herself from falling once again, but otherwise not caring which way she went. Small rises of the ground appeared before her, and she climbed them all, looked around, and finding everything the same, walked on. The wind rising and falling and singing in her ears began to plague her, somehow, and she brushed with her free hand about her head as if shooing it away.

But its crying and sobbing kept on and on and on, until Junie began to think she would go mad from the incessant noise of it, and she set down the juniper and clapped both her hands over her ears. The sound receded a bit, but still kept on, and when Junie took her hands away again it seemed to rush into her ears with renewed force. But now — wait — she stopped and tried to hear through the wind, for now there was a new voice added to its wail. Yes, there was something, and now that she had fixed on it, Junie realized it must have been there all along. Another crying, a crying like an inner voice of the wind, and almost indistinguishable from it. Almost — but now Junie had heard it, she heard it clearly. And the sound of that voice brought feeling back to her once again, for it was the most desperate and horrible sound she had ever heard, a sound like an animal dying slowly, in great pain.

She went towards it, for although it pained and frightened her to hear it, still it was the voice of a living thing in that empty place, and it drew her. She went astray, at first, for the sound of the voice was blown and carried away by the larger voice of the wind, so that it was difficult to place where it was coming from. But in a sudden lull of the wind she heard it again, behind her, and she turned and followed it to the other side of one of the little hills.

She must not have been thinking clearly yet, or perhaps she wasn't thinking at all, or she might not have rushed headlong towards that voice. As it was, she didn't stop to give herself time to consider, and so was unprepared for what she saw. She came upon him from behind, and in the darkness didn't see him clearly until she was nearly upon him.

He was crouched down on the ground with his back towards Junie, leaning over something he held in his hands and muttering strangely. Junie at first saw only the dark shape of his huddled form and a gleam from whatever he held in his hands, strangely bright in the darkness. She stood there behind him, resisting an urge to run away, peered through the gloom and tried to make out what he was saying.

"It won't, it won't, I can't — " he said, his voice rising in anger or despair. "Damn the thing! How can I? It must, it must — " His hands passed over what he was holding and he held it up. Junie caught a very brief glimpse of a frightened face, took a moment to know it was her own, and realized he was holding a mirror that had shown her her own reflection as he waved it wildly back and forth. She took a step or two backwards.

The man, still not seeing Junie behind him, laughed a little, and Junie winced at the sound. "No butter from this cream," he said, mockingly, "though churned for a thousand years. No turning back, now, it won't turn, it won't turn back. Do you hear me?" he shouted again as he had before, into the teeth of the wind. "I can't do it, our lake has dried up, there's no more water, no water anywhere." He turned the mirror over and over in his hands, and Junie watched, fascinated, trying to remember something that was teasing at the edge of her mind.

All at once the man gave a great cry and hurled the mirror away from him. Junie, remembering in that instant, cried out, "No, don't!" and heard the mirror crash and splinter, and in the same moment shrank away as the man wheeled around to face her.

He had fallen silent as she spoke, and remained silent now, but very slowly weaved towards her, squinting to see who had spoken, to see what voice had come to break his solitary raving.

Junie hid her face in her hands as he loomed towards her, all her fear of the old man in the portrait coming back, coming back stronger than ever now that she finally had to face him in the flesh. She cowered and hid her eyes, waiting to be struck or beaten or cursed by the horrible old enchanter. But nothing happened.

He was still there; Junie could hear him breathing in ragged gasps through the wailing wind. But he seemed simply to stand there before her, waiting perhaps, like her, to see what would happen. And again through her fear, Junie began to feel foolish, and realized that whatever awful fate might await her, she would rather face it boldly than stand whimpering, afraid to look.

Very slowly she took her hands away from her eyes. And the first thing she saw, as she blinked and swallowed, was the pair of green boots. There, a few feet away from her, standing on the grass, were the green boots as she had seen them and dreamed them so many times before. In spite of herself she smiled a little at the sight of them. It was like seeing an old friend.

And then she looked up, and met the face above hers that was waiting to see her own. It was the face of an old man, lined and haggard with ages of anguish — exactly the same as the face in the portrait. But it didn't frighten her. She was amazed, but when she saw him peering at her, as bewildered as herself, head on one side, she saw in a kind of flash that all her fear of this poor man had been a mistake, something of her own making, that he was anxious and in despair, but not frightening. Never frightening at all.

Afterwards, she was embarrassed, she wished she had thought of something better to say, something noble and profound, and she blushed for months whenever she remembered it. For the only thing she could think of to say to him, now that she finally met him face to face, was, "I like your boots."

He glanced down at the boots himself when she said this, and he shook his head as if he didn't really believe what he was seeing, as if he thought Junie was a kind of mirage or illusion.

"Demons, now," he said, to himself rather than to Junie. "Demons come to taunt me, too." And he turned away from Junie and passed his hand over his eyes, wearily. And then he began to wander away, stumbling like a man lost in a desert and dying of thirst and of the teeming visions inside his own brain.

But Junie knew now what she must do. She was almost elated, freed from the last clinging remnants of her own fear, and she felt light and shining as a bubble. She snatched up the little juniper, glanced at it ruefully and said, "Sorry for all the rushing around, juniper tree. Soon you'll be planted in one spot again, safe and sound." Then she hurried over to where the broken mirror lay in fragments on the ground, and carefully picked up as many of the broken pieces as she could, trying not to cut her fingers on their sharp edges. And then she hastened after the man's footsteps, still not far away.

"I'm not a demon," she called out after him as she ran. "I haven't come to torment you! I've come to help you."

But he didn't even turn his head at the sound of her voice. He merely brushed his hands over his ears, as Junie had earlier tried to brush away the sound of the wind. He began to walk a little faster, but Junie stepped up her own pace, too, determined not to lose sight of him.

When she saw him slow his pace again and look down at the ground around him, Junie stopped and watched to see what he would do. He glanced back and saw her standing there, and she tried to smile, but he turned away shuddering, evidently still convinced she was a ghost or a vision.

He knelt and began to gather together some small objects that were lying on the ground. Junie inched closer to see what they were.

"Instantly, instantly," he was saying in a kind of chant. "Make a shape and presto! Topiary!" And then he laughed his hollow, mocking laugh again and sat down heavily on the ground. Junie crept closer still.

He had the small green plasticine shapes lined up in front of him and he picked them up and moved them around like a little boy playing with tin soldiers. Junie watched him, an immense pity rising up in her, as he set the little shapes into a circle, now a square, now a line again, muttering, "No more topiary tree, no more topiary tree," over and over and over again.

"And I thought there was no garden," Junie whispered to herself. But this was it. She was in the garden after all, but it was the garden decayed and crumbled into a wilderness again, gone back to all its original bits and pieces, inanimate, lifeless, now that Miss Quarterberry was gone and its guardian tree destroyed. And he had been here — for how long? — trying to bring it to life again. It didn't bear thinking about. Junie looked down at the broken mirror she held, and thought, This is the lake — I'm holding a lake in my hands.

Softly she went up to the old man where he still sat fumbling with the tiny topiary shapes, and said, "But there is. Look, a new topiary tree." For she knew at last what the phrase meant. The juniper, the one live tree in all the garden, was the one true topiary tree without ever having to be cut or trimmed or shaped at all. Just itself, just its own shape was enough to keep everything else in place. And if it had worked once, it might work again.

He had started at the sound of her voice, and he looked at the little juniper with the same look of puzzled bewilderment as he had given Junie before. He made to stand and walk away from her again but Junie said, "Oh, please, please don't run away again." He paused, and Junie went on. "Just listen to me for a minute, please? If you still think I'm a demon or a ghost, you can leave again and I won't follow you any more, I promise. But first, listen, please." She held her breath. And then, hugely relieved, she saw him settle back down on the ground and stare sullenly straight in front of him.

Junie sat down opposite him and looked at the little topiary shapes. "I remember when she made these." He looked at her when she said this, but looked away again at once. "I've come from her, you know," she went on, urgency growing in her voice. "She asked me to come, to try to find the way in for her, because she couldn't get here any more. She couldn't get back in. But she tried." Junie looked at the man imploringly. "She wants to come back here, back to you."

"Who's she?" he barked out, and Junie quailed. Perhaps it was too late after all, perhaps he was too far gone into madness and despair to remember. But then she caught a sly, distrustful gleam in his eyes and saw that he was testing her.

"Miss Quarterberry," she said quietly. "Rosamund Quarterberry."

"Hah," laughed the old man. "Of course. Demons know, demons know the answers. They live in here," he said, tapping his skull with one long finger. "They know all the worst things to say, all the right answers."

"I'm not a demon," Junie repeated patiently. "My name is June Elizabeth Summers, but Miss Quarterberry calls me Juniper Tree."

He looked straight at her again, and said, "Go on."

Junie took a breath. Then she reached slowly into her pocket and pulled out the symbol. She held it out to him on the palm of her hand. "Look," she said. "She gave this to me. I think I know why, now. To prove to you that I came from her."

He looked at her for a long moment, intent as a cat, and then shifted his gaze to the symbol in her hand. He reached out and picked it up from her palm, gingerly, as if it might burn him, and then began to stroke it with one finger. "Her key," he whispered, a change coming into his voice. "Her key." And he rummaged in his own clothes and produced the other half of the symbol, the matching half that made it into one whole circle.

And Junie watched, entranced, as he lay the two halves side by side on the ground and gently pushed them together. They fitted, of course, perfectly, but both Junie and the old man gasped when they saw the broken edges begin to melt and flow into one another, and a soft blue-green light shining around the symbol like a halo as the two halves fused together, and made one unbroken circle once again.

The man looked up at Junie as if he was seeing her for the first time. And when he spoke, his voice was changed, becoming stronger and younger and almost musical in its resonance with every new word. "That is the first — the first magic that has happened in this place," he said, "since she has been gone."

Junie smiled.

"And you?" he said wonderingly. "Who are you?"

"I'm just her friend," answered Junie.

"And you have come . . . "

"To help," she said. "To try and help. We have to plant the new juniper," she went on, taking advantage of his increasing clarity.

But he dropped his head and laughed his mocking laugh again. "Past planting, this place," he said. "Nothing grows in the dark, except nightmares."

"But it isn't as dark now," Junie protested. "Look." The sky was lightening in the east, and Junie could see the man's face more and more clearly. He raised his heavy head and looked at the paling sky wearily, like someone who hadn't slept in years and years.

"Dawn," he said, acknowledging the light.

Junie watched him curiously. "Your face is changing," she said. "Here, look." And she handed him a small cracked piece of mirror so he could see himself. Remarkably docile now, he took the fragment and looked at his own ravaged face in the broken glass. After a moment he looked back up at Junie, wonderingly.

"There used to be a garden here," he said. "But no more. One tree doesn't make a garden."

"Yes," said Junie. "Yes, it does. Here, it does."

After this, Junie didn't think much any more, or talk much. She felt as if she were watching herself from a long way away, passively, and it wasn't necessary to explain anything or discuss anything at all. The man continued to protest, but even as he protested he did what Junie asked, and showed her where the first juniper tree had been planted. There was nothing there now — it had long since decayed and rotted back into the earth.

And when Junie knelt and began to dig, with her hands, since there was nothing else, the man knelt and began to dig, too, silenced by Junie's silent resolve. And as they dug Junie saw his hands grow stronger and more sure, until she stopped altogether and let his greater strength finish the job.

As she loosened the little juniper gently from its pot and lowered it into its hole, Junie had one moment of uncertainty. It was hard, after all, to leave it here, and she touched its branches gently in farewell. "Remember," she told it softly.

"I will remember," said the man, trying to smile at her. "We both will." He touched the branches of the juniper as well, and then gently took Junie's hand in his own. "We will all remember," he said quietly, and looked at her with grateful, haunted eyes.

And then, feeling nothing at all but exhaustion, she watched as the man, not so old now, but never to be truly young again, placed the symbol at the base of the tree. As its blue-green gleam vanished under the soil, Junie blinked, and was gone.

19

The End

Marcus wanted all the details. But Junie was past telling, and she lay back beside Victoria on the grass and dozed, smiling. "I'll try, Marcus," she said. "But not now."

"But just tell me if you made it. Did you make it into the garden?" persisted Marcus with eager, envious eyes.

"Yes."

"And how was it?" he said.

"It wasn't — it wasn't how I expected it to be."

Nothing was how she expected it to be. She didn't feel noble, or triumphant, or even very happy. She still didn't know. She didn't know for sure if Miss Quarterberry had got back into the garden. She felt empty, and tired, and uncertain. But the magic was gone, the bright hovering sense of something wonderful that had played through the summer days. The magic was gone, and this alone made her feel Miss Quarterberry must be gone too.

Willikins lay purring on Junie's chest in the mornings, now. Either he couldn't talk any more, or Junie just couldn't hear him. She couldn't tell which.

Restless and still unsatisfied, Junie walked up and down the streets until she gathered courage to go to Miss Quarterberry's house. She couldn't tell if she longed to see the familiar face still there, or feared to. But at Number 13 Mulberry Street, a *For Sale* sign stood on the lawn. Agnes answered the door. Not knowing what to say, Junie asked if Miss Quarterberry was selling.

"Heavens, no," replied Agnes. "This is my house. Always has been. True enough, I've rented a room or two to a visiting librarian from time to time, but I'm retiring now. Too big, this place. Too complicated." She leant down and winked and laid her finger against her nose in quite her old manner. "Read any good books lately, Juniper Tree?" she asked, and then chuckled and began to close the door.

"But is she here?" whispered Junie desperately.

Agnes peered around the door again and looked at her curiously. "Why, you ought to know," she said. Junie shook her head.

"No, my dear," said Agnes, a sad smile on her face. "She ain't here."

Fiona, after a few days, noticed the absence of the potted juniper, and asked Junie about it. Junie said, "Oh, I gave it away. I gave it to somebody who needed a juniper, especially."

Just as Junie was beginning to give up hope of ever knowing what had become of Miss Quarterberry, in her book the spidery handwriting appeared once more. Above the *Juniper Tree* Junie watched, one day, as an invisible hand wrote slowly and carefully,

Fare well

And then the writing faded and the page bloomed into colour before her eyes, and for a short moment Junie saw them together in the blooming garden, saw the little juniper flanked by lawns and flowers, and then at last she knew, and was satisfied, and she closed the book.

Melody Collins Thomason has long been fascinated
by children's books, particularly tales of magic. "It
is the magic of books that draws me both to read
them and to write them. . . . It means both seeing
beyond the surface of things and sensing the
possibilities there."

Melody, a graduate of University of Toronto, lives
in Guelph, Ontario, with her cat Sebastian, also
known as Sausage, and her husband, a zoologist.
When she is not busy writing (she is currently
working on her third novel), she indulges her
passions for ancient Greek, seventeenth century
poetry, gardening, classical music and "occasional
attacks of poetry writing."